Praise for *Word Witch*

"With tenderness and thoughtfulness, Kate Belew, a dynamic and experienced Word Witch herself, guides readers through the powerful magic of storytelling, using our words to seek out and honor our Truth and craft spells that change the world, building our reality one letter, one word, one page at a time."

—Amy Torok, coauthor of *Missing Witches* and *New Moon Magic*, and cohost of the *Missing Witches* podcast

"Whether you identify as a writer, a witch, or a honey-tongued poet, this book is an essential addition to your library."

—Danielle Dulsky, author of *The Night House* and *The Holy Wild*

"*Word Witch* is both spell and guide, a weaving of Kate's decades-long journey as a poet, scholar, and practicing Witch. Rooted in literary study and lived magical practice, it offers intuitive exercises, foundational teachings, and profound stories from Kate's own path. The book meets you where you are: a grounding start for new Word Witches, a creative catalyst for seasoned writers, and a nourishing balm for those in need of inspiration."

—Xenia Marie Ross Viray, imagination healer and founder of Myths of Creation

"*Word Witch* is both a celebration of creative expression and a step-by-step guide to enchanting writing practices old and new. By weaving together storytelling, automatic writing exercises, and journaling prompts, readers learn to craft 'altars of language' and summon their inner Word Witch."

—Kristin Lisenby, author of *Little Witch Tales: Telling the Bees* and cohost of the *Magick & Alchemy* podcast

"The soft, fierce potency of putting pen to page, the mystical alchemy of creativity, the transformation of the base material of ideas into literary gold—*Word Witch* explores innumerable ways to harness the power of written language. Drawing on Belew's personal experience as seeker, teacher, and guide, this richly dense grimoire celebrates the integration of ritual, intention, and spellwork into creative expression and ultimately offers a deeply thoughtful exploration of the practice of writing as a magical act."

—Jessica Hundley, editor and author of *The Library of Esoterica*

WORD WITCH

WORD WITCH

How to Call Upon and Cultivate the Creative Magic Within You

Kate Belew

balance
New York Boston

Balance
Hachette Book Group
1290 Avenue of the Americas
New York, NY 10104
GCP-Balance.com
@GCPBalance

First Edition: October 2025

Balance is an imprint of Grand Central Publishing. The Balance name and logo are registered trademarks of Hachette Book Group, Inc.

The publisher is not responsible for websites (or their content) that are not owned by the publisher.

Balance books may be purchased in bulk for business, educational, or promotional use. For information, please contact your local bookseller or the Hachette Book Group Special Markets Department at special.markets@hbgusa.com.

Print book interior design by Bart Dawson

Library of Congress Cataloging-in-Publication Data has been applied for.

ISBNs: 9780306836824 (paper over board), 9780306836831 (ebook)

Printed in the United States of America

LSC-C

Printing 1, 2025

This book is dedicated to the Word Witches.

Writing with you is an honor. This is dedicated to your voices, stories, magic, enchantment, and the possibility of making a better world—to all our imaginations. To my husband, Cody, and dog, Banjo, because I love you. And to my younger self in the fairy garden, longing to write books and move to New York City, this is for you.

CONTENTS

Foreword xiii

Chapter One: *Word Witches* 1

Chapter Two: *What Is an Altar?* 23

Chapter Three: *The Foundation* 33

Chapter Four: *Air* 59

Chapter Five: *Fire* 75

Chapter Six: *Water* 95

Chapter Seven: *Earth* 115

Chapter Eight: *Spirit* 149

A Final Blessing, for Now 187

Acknowledgments 189
Appendix A: The Four Steps to Creating a Writing Ritual 193
Appendix B: Astrological Season Writing Prompts 197
Appendix C: Full Moon Poetry Prompts 223
Appendix D: New Moon Poetry Prompts 237
Appendix E: A Ritual: Calling Your Energy Back 251
Notes 255
Index 261
About the Author 269

WORD WITCH

FOREWORD

Kate Belew, in her newest book, *Word Witch: How to Call Upon and Cultivate the Creative Magic Within You,* makes it clear that she is calling out to you, personally, and that in her view, writing and magic are utterly intertwined. She notes the connection between "spell" and "spelling," and provides us with three guiding beliefs for any Word Witch: "Everyone is creative. Everything is connected. Writing is magic."

Kate warmly invites each reader, in her distinctive voice, to access the writing magic she assures us we hold within ourselves. Then, throughout the course of *Word Witch,* she shows us how to do it. How to let go. How to listen. How to connect through ritual. How to experiment. How to dive into an array of seasonal, astrological, and other writing prompts she provides. And, above all, how to open to possibility.

Belew links us to the lineage of writers as spellcasters, those who make the intangible tangible, and to the support and power we gain from cultivating our connection to the magic of Earth and the living reality of the elements. She encourages us to inhabit our bodies, and our unique lives, in order to empower our authentic expression, with full awareness of the dangerous moment we are living in as a collective. She writes: "Possibility is a healing force in the world."

Knowing Kate's Witch spirit and generous personality, and already being familiar with her writing, I expected this book to be good. I assumed I would put it up on the shelf with my other favorite books by writers on writing: *Writing Down the Bones* by Natalie Goldberg, Philip Pullman's *Daemon Voices*, and others. We writers love to hear tips on storytelling, on how to write when we feel dry or stuck, and on how to believe in ourselves as writers. I imagined *Word Witch* would be poetic, helpful, and insightful.

I couldn't have known how truly exceptional it would be, but it is. Kate's book reads like an inspiring love letter to the storyteller in each of us, affirming our right, and indeed our need, to write, to weave magic with our words, to reclaim ourselves as we lift our voices to express who we are, how we see, and to better our world. It is apparent on every page of *Word Witch* that Kate Belew believes in us, and in the value of our writing, whether we have published books ourselves or are scribbling on the backs of napkins.

We get a glimpse of how the author grew into a Word Witch in the opening chapter. Kate's love of language began before she could write. She used to dictate poems to her mom, who would record them for her! Kate charms us effortlessly, drawing us into her magic as she describes herself—a child in love with libraries full of books, plants, unicorns, fairies, and magic. She invites us into her home to meet her grandma and grandpa, and writes about their friend who told her mysterious stories that still excite her imagination today. Kate writes, "Writing allows me to be all my ages at once," and follows that with the declaration, "Writing is magic for many reasons, but one of those reasons is because it's an act of time traveling." She says that Word Witches are dreamers who "carry curiosity in their hearts...and ask questions to better understand the world around them," then adds, "I tell my story because I want you to know whose voice speaks to you as you peruse these pages. We are together in a ritual."

Ah, yes, *Word Witch* is an invitation into a cocreative ritual. The book itself, *Word Witch*, grew over years from a lovely little workbook into the authoritative book you now hold in your hands. As Kate's mentor on the Green Witch path, I see that she grew this book as she grew herself, authentically, over time, with ongoing passionate dedication, focused attention, and by doing the work, both mundane and magical, which is simple, but rarely easy!

Kate succinctly captures the essence of her book with these words: "This book...shows you step-by-step how to build a magical practice in your life and cultivate a creative, full, and authentic life through writing."

The author asserts, "Word Witches are spellcasters of language." It is impossible to define what a Witch is, for as Kate acknowledges, there is "no one way to be a Witch." Yet, I agree with her that we can assert the essential truth that witches "live by sacred cycles" of nature, "honor the web of life on our planet," and "are committed to justice." I also love that she says, "Witchcraft is a resounding yes to the ritual of being alive."

In the part of *Word Witch* where she most clearly invokes our magical work together, Kate shares her associations with each of the elements, as well as her understanding of how we are not only made of these ancient elements but how they infuse our work and lives. She teaches the reader how to magically cast a circle, so as to create a sacred container in which to work, and connects each of the elements to particular aspects of the craft of writing.

Word Witch is filled with imagination-inducing writing prompts for new and full moons, astrological seasons, and more. Everything in this book is designed to get you writing! And to inspire you to live with authentic passion.

Kate Belew invites us to Word Witchery as a path of liberation, beckoning us to make our voices heard, inviting us to become part of the community of writers and to make our world a more joyful and just place.

There is so much wisdom, wit, and warmth in this book; I suspect that, like me, you will want to keep *Word Witch* within easy reach, to inspire your unique writing magic. Blessed Be!

—Robin Rose Bennett, storyteller, Green Witch, author of *The Gift of Healing Herbs: Plant Medicines and Home Remedies for a Vibrantly Healthy Life*, *Healing Magic: A Green Witch Guidebook to Conscious Living*, *A Green Witch's Pocket Book of Wisdom–Big Little Life Tips*, and *The Young Green Witch's Guide to Plant Magic: Rituals and Recipes from Nature*

Chapter One

WORD WITCHES

Word Witches have existed since the beginning of time. As long as there have been humans, there have been storytellers, stories, and those making magic and casting spells with words. The occult, magic, and spells can be found in our most ancient examples of language.

Word Witches have lived in every culture, across every civilization on earth. *Why?* Because humans are hardwired for stories and rituals. They gather us together, deliver us through the night, bring us around the fire and the hearth, and are proof of our survival. They say, "We were here," *which is a blessing.*

Every poet, writer, author, memoirist, and lyricist who loves the earth, believes in possibility, and embraces mystery has a story of their journey as a Word Witch. *And this is mine.*

My journey into Word Witchery began before I could write on my own. I used to dictate poems to my mom, and she would record them for me. They were about unicorns, fairies, plants, and magic—my first loves in this lifetime on earth.

I have always been a reader. I spent many summers in my childhood at the Marshall Public Library, in my hometown in Michigan, participating in summer reading challenges. I remember reading *Poetry for Young People: Emily Dickinson* with my dad when I was eight. Dickinson taught me about hope and feathers and bogs and how delightful it was to be a nobody. I saw her concise and specific word choices as amulets, and sacred objects, something to grasp on to and keep treasured. She gave me, among many things, the em dash—this lingering piece of grammatical magic, like a wand extended onto the page. She gave me the poem "I'm Nobody! Who Are You?" It was the first poem I memorized, and I still know it by heart. From the past, across the page, she invited me onto the path of writing.

From Emily Dickinson, to Edgar Allan Poe, to Judy Blume, Monica Furlong, Tamora Pierce, and Bruce Coville, I immersed myself in the worlds of authors and writers. There is a hidden secret to our magic in what we loved in childhood. Heaving the dictionary onto my bedroom floor, I would investigate any word on the page that didn't yet feel familiar when I came across it. When I began to write for myself, I kept journals, diaries, and scraps of poems on loose pages. This wasn't a practice I needed to be taught, though I was encouraged by my favorite characters like Jo March, Harriet the Spy, and Cam Jansen, in books and on the screen, the quiet ones, the ones who loved libraries, and the ones who always had their noses in a book.

My parents and older family members reinforced the magic and power of words. My dad's mom, Joan, was a librarian.

Whenever we visited her in Dowagiac, she would read to my siblings and me and check out movies for us like *The Last Unicorn* and *The Phantom Tollbooth* from the library. These stories encouraged and cultivated my imagination. They placed me in the world of stories and magic. They asked questions of me, introduced me to the idea of mystery, and showed me that creativity was a relationship that I would need to tend to for my whole life. I was invited along, and I accepted. Who was I to turn down the fantastical, mythical world that I believed then, and still know now to be possible? I love these stories today, treasures from my childhood and reminders of the importance of these tales.

✸ *Word Witches are dreamers.* ✸

Some of my first writings were questions. I would leave notes to the fairies living in the garden outside my mom's house. After school, I would tuck them into the houses made of sticks that my best friend Jules and I, and my sister, would dutifully create for them. We knowingly built these structures under the white birch tree and the cedar in the fairy garden. We inherently knew that we loved ferns. These letters wanted to know everything about fairy land, such as whether or not I could visit, and if so, what the rules might be, and what happened to them during Michigan winters.

✸ *Word Witches carry curiosity in their hearts. They believe and ask questions to better understand the world around them.* ✸

During these years, I lived down the street from my mom's dad, Pop Pop, and Grandma Lucy. They kept an extensive library at home, and whenever I would go and have tea on the porch with my grandma and her friends, they would ask me what I was reading and tell me about their favorites in return. The books on my grandparents' shelves detailed the imaginary worlds I dreamed about day and night. They spoke about Thunder Cake and forbidden doors, young women who traveled to the realms of the unicorns, women who dressed as men to become knights, dragons who weren't cruel but misunderstood, and Witches who found solace in the woods.

This is also where I encountered divination for the first time. My grandma's friend Karla, a woman who owned a bookstore in another city in Michigan, first brought this magic into my life. Karla would come to my grandma's house with her tarot cards, along with strange and surreal presents, and antiques. She would send my sister and me letters detailing the lore around these items, and she always had a story to share with us whenever she visited, and these stories felt like sacred secrets. I still keep a jar with a lock of her hair (she said it belonged to Rapunzel), a white lamp that was said to house a spirit, and a gold heart locket that was charmed for the witchcraft of love spells. Karla knew that these secrets were the currency of childhood and that mystery taught from a young age would be mystery embraced forever.

Childhood lore lives forever.
✸ *Word Witches have imaginations free* ✸
to run wild across the landscape.

I wrote my first poem in 2003 about an oak tree that fell in my grandparents' yard.

I remember grieving over the body of the oak, running the block home, compelled suddenly to find paper and pen, and writing:

The oak tree stands a minute longer
The breeze makes it sway
I hear a crack, the whole world rumbles
It's lying on its side
The old oak tree has lived its life
Stood its purpose
The oak tree sways no more

I don't know where the poem came from inside me, but I knew I needed to write it. My mom then framed it and hung it on the wall of my grandparents' house, along with some photos of me with my siblings and the oak. These early childhood experiences showed me that time could be marked through writing, grief alchemized. Whole new worlds could be made accessible to me through writing.

Since then I've dedicated my life, my work, and my path to the written word.

Writing allows me to be all my ages at once.

Writing is magic for many reasons,
but one of those reasons is because
it's an act of time traveling.

I'll share some of these stories, of my journey as a Word Witch, throughout this book, and hopefully, they'll be a helpful guide for you to follow as you build your writing life.

These stories come from a lifetime of different experiences. I've completed residencies and fellowships (including one where I slept for a week in a refurbished chicken coop in a holler outside Knoxville—thank you to Sundress Publications), received an MFA from Sarah Lawrence, published poems, created zines, written books, launched a podcast, and taught in prison, middle schools, high schools, libraries, with artists, with Witches, with sacred collaborators and friends, online, in community gardens, a church, art galleries, elementary schools, and retreats across the globe.

The magic of writing can be found anywhere (and can take you anywhere!). All you have to do is offer your attention and cultivate and care for your creative life as the wild animal that it is.

The path of the Word Witch is long and winding. Even as I write now, my path continues to unfurl, and I'm beyond grateful. It appears under my feet. I have never regretted my English degree. I wish I'd had the words to answer this question while studying English as an undergrad at Kalamazoo College, but now I do.

"What will you do with an English degree?" people would ask.

"*Anything*," I'd now tell them.

I tell my story because I want you to know whose voice speaks to you as you peruse these pages. We are together in a ritual.

This is the hand I reach across the page to offer you. I tell my story so you can feel empowered to share yours, too. And all of the other stories waiting to come from you.

I created this book because it's the book I have needed to read since I was young. Possibility is a healing force in the world. An open door is a gift. Many of us (including myself) wait for an invitation, for permission to create something, but we need to take a step across the threshold and create the invitation for ourselves. This book is a guide on that path of reclamation and self-determination. It shows you step-by-step how to build a magical practice in your life and cultivate a creative, full, and authentic life through writing. What's at stake in this reclamation is our passion, drive, and creative lives. To claim your creative life is to live a life that is truly and uniquely yours. To be a Word Witch is to tell your stories and to listen. This book exists so that we may all thrive together.

I wrote this book for those who've attended my workshops and listened to our podcast. I wrote this book because I know there are so many Word Witches out there, wondering if they are genuinely the artists, poets, writers, or Witches they feel they are in their hearts. And I'm here to say, "Yes, you are."

Thank you for traveling on this Word Witch path with me. Now, let's begin.

Who Is a Word Witch?

First, let's define the word "Witch" (*before* we define what a "Word Witch" is). Witches are anyone—regardless of gender, sexuality, race, age, or class—who live by sacred cycles. Witches are committed to justice and reclamation; they honor the web of life on our planet, the one that we're all connected to. Witches cast spells, gather in covens, and/or craft magic in a solitary practice.

There is no one way to be a Witch.

Witches are dedicated to enchantment, awe, and possibility. They know that magic is our collective birthright and that all the magic you need can be found inside yourself and on the beautiful planet we call home. If you long to call yourself a Witch, then you *are* a Witch. "Witch" can be handed down in a long magical lineage, but this identity can also be claimed for the self.

In *Missing Witches,* Amy Torok writes, "We, as people, as Witches, as part of Nature are more verb and adjective than noun. We are not just one thing. We are nebulous, paradoxical, contradictory. We seek descriptors, not labels, wisdom over knowledge. We are whole. And Holy."[1]

Witches are wild, feral, and of the earth. Resisting definition, toward possibility. Witchcraft is a resounding yes to the ritual of being alive.

There are many ways to embody or practice your magic (and you can embody many of these approaches simultaneously). People call themselves "Green Witches" when they are herbalists and study a plant-inspired path; "Kitchen Witches" when they love to spend time cooking and infusing magic into recipes and medicines; "Hedge Witches" when they dedicate their practice to the liminal, divination, and the otherworld; "Eclectic Witches" when they like to study myriad different magical topics and want to defy all definitions; and "Word Witches" when they are writers and authors and like to channel their magic through the written word (to name a few). These terms can be fun ways to announce yourself to the world, just as it's often fun to discover new things about yourself. They aren't prescriptive, necessary, or just one thing, but they are invitations, nonhierarchical clubs and communities to explore. In this text, I refer to myself as a Green Witch because of the Wise Wild Woman Tradition of Healing apprenticeship I completed with herbalist, author, and magic maker Robin Rose Bennett, as well as a Word Witch. The word "Witch" itself also suits me just fine.

Who *you* are deep inside always, *always* transcends a singular label. And if the word "Witch" doesn't resonate with you for whatever reason you hold in your heart, I'm here to say that's okay, too. Maybe you'll change your mind. Who knows. Magic can still be found in these pages, and whatever magic, ritual, or practice you'd like to develop can come from that place.

After all, Word Witches are not rule followers. They are forever questioning and exploring and pushing at the boundaries of what is possible. That is what the imagination is. The only absolute path is honoring all the paths, so we travel them together here. The most important part is that you believe.

A quote I treasure is from the novel *Even Cowgirls Get the Blues* by Tom Robbins, the first book my husband gave me when we started dating; it brings me back to myself in saying, "disbelief in magic can force a poor soul into believing in government and business."[2] *Magic is important.* Government and business are important, *sure,* but I don't want to give them my heart and soul, my very beliefs in the world. That's for me and magic. *I believe in magic.*

Enchantment is important. Storytelling is important. And it's important how we approach and honor these practices. In the words of poet Muriel Rukeyser, "The universe is made of stories, not of atoms."[3] Stories are our commonality, our altar, and the proof that we are alive or ever lived at all. We are stitches in the sewing thread of the stories that we read, take in, and then pass on.

In thinking about telling stories and reclamation, I often turn to the work of Risa Dickens and Amy Torok and their book *Missing Witches.* In the introduction to their gorgeous collection of historical investigation, curiosity, magic, and celebration, they quote Amanda Yates Garcia, saying,

> It matters whose stories get told; it matters how we tell them. Imagination matters. Our connections to one another matter, as does the pleasure we take in our experience. Witches stand in solidarity with those already doing this work, because people have been doing this work since humans first appeared on the surface of the earth. Now we listen to them, we participate, we use techniques of the healer, the poet, the artist, the scholar, the cunning folk to re-enchant the world.[4]

Imagination is part of our inherent magic. We reenchant the world by strengthening our relationship with this part of ourselves. Though we might practice in a solitary space—at a desk, in a coffee shop, in a park, or realistically on a bed (like I am as I write this now)—we are writing alongside everyone who deeply loves and cares for this craft, everyone who ever has in the past and everyone who will in the future. By studying other writers' ideas and the writing of Word Witches, we can develop and expand our theories, perspectives, and paths.

The paths are winding, Witch!
But you will always know the way
to go for you.

This is a lifelong journey, one of working with the imagination, telling the stories, and listening to the stories that must be told, voices from the depths of the earth, crafted by all of us, all over the world. When you write, you join a lineage. When you write, you actively participate in the magic of being alive. When you write, you prove that the intangible can be made tangible, that story can persevere, and that the human spirit is resilient and inherently creative. The word "enchantment" itself comes from the old French *encantement,* meaning, "magical spell, song, concert, or chorus," but the root of that is related to the Latin *cantare,* "to sing."

Stories sing the soul of the world.
And Witches tell these stories.

Now, let's talk about the practice of Word Witchery.

Word Witches are spellcasters of language. They are storytellers, poets, writers, and ritualists who know that writing anything is a form of channeling: spirits, ancestors, collective dreams, and their most authentic and surprising selves. Many Word Witches spent their childhoods reading paperback novels by flashlight. They conjure up poems with their magic wands and their pens. Word Witches love music and write lyrics down on napkins and notebook covers. They love making things. They have a worn-out library card or a stack of books on their nightstand. They listen to audiobooks while they walk. Word Witches have a favorite pen. They keep a dream of publishing something in their heart. They submit their writing to journals. They run journals. They collaborate with other Word Witches. Word Witches might share at an open mic or keep their words secret and tucked into a journal.

Above all else, Word Witches love a story and a storyteller.

✸ *And you might be a Word Witch, too.* ✸

I remember first calling myself a Word Witch out loud in a conversation with photographer and artist Frances F. Denny in 2016. Frances was taking photos for her project *Major Arcana: Portraits of Witches in America.*[5] We sat in the apothecary I worked in on First Street in New York City and talked about the power of writing and of language. This conversation was catalytic for me, two artists in NYC, talking about how our creativity empowers us and leads us forward on our paths.

I was still new to the city, and when I look at the photo of myself Frances took after our conversation, I now see a beginning, which makes me smile. These were the kinds of conversations I moved to the city for, and it inspired me to meet others who believed in the same possibilities I did. The people you meet on your Word Witch path are the most crucial part.

✸ *Community is a part of our creative process.* ✸

In the pages of Frances's collection, I described my magic as follows: "I am a poet by art and trade, and so I have found that my magic comes best through my words and that poems can act as sorts of spells. I am a Word Witch. Having something to say and having a voice is sometimes the toughest magic there is. It has been such a galvanizing force in my life."

Since saying these words, I have met others who have called themselves Word Witches, Poetry Witches, Art Witches, and more. It's not a singular title; it's one we all share. It was as if the same magic was whispering into our ears, begging us to write these ideas down. Witchcraft and writing come from the same place. In *Waking the Witch: Reflections on Women, Magic, and Power,* Pam Grossman writes, "Say what you will about witches, but we are a literary bunch."[6] Word Witches create with this love of literature. Word Witches love a book. To be a Word Witch is to have a deep connection to your creativity. Writing conjures. Writing makes possible. Writing makes real the world, the kind of magic that makes the etheric real, which is a spell.

So, let's cast a spell. Together, let's put our ears to the earth to hear that hum of magic that guides our pens and wands.

The Guiding Beliefs of a Word Witch

Though the title of "Word Witch" resists singular definition, here are just three beliefs and principles a Word Witch can live by; these can act as guides and as lanterns on the Word Witch path. They are simple because, sometimes, the simple spell is the most powerful.

1. Everyone is creative.
2. Everything is connected.
3. Writing is magic.

Repeat these beliefs out loud three times.

Who Is This Book For?

I am opening a door for you here, writer. I can't wait for you to step through and across this threshold. This book is for you whether you already consider yourself a writer, or you used to write and you haven't for a while, or you've never written in your life but long to tell a story.

I wrote this book for you if you want to infuse your life with daily rituals; discover the world of enchantment, witchcraft, and magic; or add a new dimension to your practice as a practicing Witch. This book is for the young, the old, and everyone in between because we can all learn from one another, write with one another, and create in community and togetherness.

So whether you consider yourself a Witch, a writer, somewhere in between, or neither of the above, if you long to discuss the craft (pun intended), *you are welcome here.*

Word Witches know that magic is for everyone and everyone is magic.

In author Stephen King's *On Writing: A Memoir of the Craft*, he said, "If you want to be a writer, you must do two things above all others: read a lot and write a lot. There's no way around these two things that I'm aware of, no shortcut."[7]

Every time I teach a writing workshop, the inevitable moment comes when I inform the participants that to be a writer, *you must write.*

To clarify, I don't mean that you must *always* be writing or that everything you write must be productive or profound. Sometimes artists take long breaks in between making. I call breaks like this my "collecting phase," where I gather all my information, musings, and adventures into a basket as if I am out foraging. Sometimes it's essential to head into the woods and fill your basket before coming home to create something new.

But writing, at its heart, is a muscle, an impulse, a dance. The words live within us, waiting to come out, to be coaxed out, to be committed to. Writing is a tool, and to devote time and energy to the task of it is essential.

It is a *conjuring.*

It's not a coincidence that both witchcraft and writing are called "the craft."

Wherever you start on the journey won't be where you end up, but that's exactly the point. Ten years, six months, a week from now, you'll be glad you started this journey *today*. After recording 140 podcast episodes of *Magick & Alchemy*,[8] a podcast by Tamed Wild that I cocreate with my cohost Kristin Lisenby, I recently reviewed my notes from our very first episode four years ago, discovering just how far we've come. Our voices were shaky, unsure, and hopeful in that first episode, but we never would have arrived to today without saying that first word. This book began with a single mark and now it exists in your hands. The first step, that first mark, can be intimidating, but it's so important that you do it.

Begin with one step, or in this case, a single Word document on a laptop, a single piece of paper, or a page in your journal.

While you read this book, I want you to write. And I want you to write through ritual. Word Witches live at the intersection of these words (writing and ritual), or rather, the crossroads, to draw upon an old, old archetype. The crossroads is a place where things come together and things pass through. It is the fringe, a portal, the liminal, which is a constant source and support for our creative lives. (We'll talk more about that later!)

In each chapter you'll find exercises and rituals to guide you through this work. They will be our gathering place. When we rest here at the intersection of words and magic, our creative practices can be built from the ground up.

✸ *So, write we will.* ✸

What You Can Expect

Expectations are strange, and we're often told not to have them, or they can lead to disappointment. I think this can be true, but I also believe that setting our expectations can help to keep us excited and aware about the paths that we are taking and choosing.

I don't know for sure how this work and practice will ripple out in your life, but I do know that the following musings, missives, rituals, and Word Witchery have the power and the possibility to bring about change in our lives.

From my experience, you might feel more flow, more creativity, a sense of connectedness and presence, and a ritual practice you can return to for the rest of your life as a writer. Every time you come to the page, you can expect that things will be different. This is magic. *Change is magic.* The possibility for things to be made different in our lives is powerful, and this is something that waits for you on the pages ahead.

A Note on My Lineage

When I write or speak about my lineage, I think of my creative lineage, my magical and healing lineage, and my family lineage. These three aspects, woven together, are where I teach from and have been a great source of education and inspiration.

My creative lineage is every writer I've ever loved, every person I've ever had a workshop with, every professor who has mentored me or offered their wisdom to me, and any books I have read and enveloped into my understanding of the creative arts. I speak more about these teachers and guides in my acknowledgments. Lineage works two ways, and I also include my students in this lineage because every time I teach, I learn from the incredible writers I have the honor of facilitating for and with.

As for my magical lineage, I completed a three-year Green Witch and herbalism apprenticeship in the Wise Wild Woman Tradition of Healing with Robin Rose Bennett. This apprenticeship fostered a deep practice of connecting with the importance of magic and ritual in my life and taught me about the healing powers and wisdom teachings of plants. As I write this, I am an apprentice in her clinical practice, helping support others on their healing journeys.

Ancestrally, my mom's grandparents emigrated from Germany to Detroit, and my father's family emigrated from Poland and France, eventually to the Midwest. I carry their faces, bodies, and stories in my body and blood. I think of my European roots when I tell stories. The land where New York and Michigan are carved into borders has made me who I am, and that land itself is a part of my lineage as a writer and Witch.

I would also like to honor the original and still present caretakers of the land where I work. In New York City, this includes the Lenape, and in Michigan, the Anishinaabe.[9] *Thank you to those who came before me and who will come after me.*

How to Read This Book

One of the most challenging parts of writing this book is telling people what they "should" do. So, instead, I offer that this is a book of what *could be* instead, a book of possibilities.

It is a door opening.

It is an invitation.

This is my offering, my altar, that you and I will meet at as I guide you through the enchanting process of deepening your relationship with your writing. Take what resonates with you; follow the threads, the prompts, and the examples that make you feel as if you are walking through a quiet forest, skipping through a meadow, or sipping tea and staring at a river. *Those* will be the best Word Witch practices for you.

Of course, I encourage you to *try* everything—at least to see if it works for you or not. I know that Witches (myself included) often resist authority figures. But, authority and author do share a root word, *autos* of Greek origin, meaning self. This is about stepping into and embracing the authentic self, the creative, the artist, the Witch. Think of me as an old friend, a companion, holding a lantern alongside you as you embark on a new creative path forward.

As for my recommendation, I'd suggest reading this book one chapter at a time and in order. For a more compressed approach, you could read one chapter each day and then practice the corresponding rituals. You could also read this book beginning on a new moon, plotting out the chapters to finish on a full moon, or vice versa. Or you could read one chapter per week. The chapters are as follows, with a schedule of how I might approach this work.

The Word Witch Journey

Week #1: What Is an Altar?
Week #2: The Foundation
Week #3: Air
Week #4: Fire
Week #5: Water
Week #6: Earth
Week #7: Spirit

Whatever you do, however you do it, take your time as you work through the exercises. Think about what it means to you to make magic and to make writing in the world. If you'd like, you can embark on this journey with a friend, a book club, or your coven and see how that impacts your process. It's always wonderful to talk about writing with others.

At the end of the chapters, you'll find a collection of writing prompts you can spend time with during each astrological season. There are also poetry prompts for every new and full moon, a step-by-step guide to creating a writing ritual, and a ritual for calling your energy back when you're feeling ungrounded or blocked in your writing practice.

I've included these so that you'll come back and visit with your Word Witch practices under the full moon's light, the shadows of the new moon, or the wonderful and different vibrant energies accompanying each astrological season. My hope is that you'll bring these to your moon circles, share them with your covens, and practice these writing rituals in your life as you follow the spiral path forward.

The Spiral Path of the Word Witch

Everything moves in spirals.

This book—much like the path of the Word Witch—is a spiral offering of scraps of writing, famous figures, Word Witches, my own experience, prompts, and rituals. These are tidal thoughts, seasonal, and cyclical. This is a collage of a writing life for Witches and writers who know that writing and living are deeply intertwined.

As Witch, activist, and the author of *The Spiral Dance: A Rebirth of the Ancient Religion of the Great Goddess* Starhawk once wrote, "Decide what is sacred to you, and put your best life energies at its service. Make that the focus of your studies, your work, the test for your pleasures, and your relationships. Don't ever let fear or craving for security turn you aside. When you serve your passion, when you are willing to risk yourself for something, your greatest creative energies are released. Hard work is required, but nothing is more joyful."[10]

Let this work be sacred to you. Let this work be hard work, joyful work. Let the words and the writing lead you, connect you, remind you, reclaim you, spiraling, spiraling.

Know that this magic is possible, probable even. We'll begin this practice, by building an altar.

You are a Word Witch.
And Word Witches build altars with language.

Chapter Two

WHAT IS AN ALTAR?

The altar is an invitation, creating a place for dedication. The word "altar" comes from the Middle English *altar,* Old English *alter,* and Latin *altarae,* which may have been related to *adolere,* meaning "burn" or "the burning places," and *altus,* meaning "high." Understanding this etymology helps us understand the power of offerings, transformation, and dedicating a space to a practice. The altar is sacred, a burning place for offerings, it is raised up.

The altar is just that—a place to dedicate your spiritual practice. It is a place made real in the world to connect you to the divine, or spirit, which can sometimes feel just beyond our physical senses, out of our fingertips' reach. In the physical realm, an altar is a place for us to bring our offerings to, where we can consecrate sacred tools, make and unmake our worlds, and pray, hoping that the divine can hear our poems and our voices in earnest.

Just as there are many different Witches, there are many different kinds of altars. You'll see altars dedicated to an ancestral line and altars created to support a specific spell. There are seasonal altars that celebrate earth-based holidays. Some altars are elaborate and contain heirlooms and treasures, while others are built entirely from found earth-crafted materials. No matter what they are made with or why they are created, the most important thing is that you find this space sacred. An altar is not just something we can see or rest our hands on in the physical plane; it exists energetically as a place we can return to again and again to draw inspiration, seek counsel, and store the seeds of our ideas.

You may be familiar with images of what altars look like from encountering them in temples, in churches, in photos, online, or in a relative's home, but try to release any preconceived notions of what an altar must have or any religious rules that keep your altar energetically small or not authentic to you. More than anything else, your altar should feel sacred to you.

Building your altar is a way to explore your spirituality, creating your connection to magic, spirit, all that is. And this is the first step into the crossroads of your ritual and writing practices.

✸ *It's your altar; you get to make the rules.* ✸

·•☽ Building an Altar ☾•·

Whenever I build a new altar, I consider my intention first. Altars don't solely work to honor, bless, or ritualize, sending magic out into the universe; they can also conjure, call, or draw in new ideas and sparks of inspiration.

My favorite altars do both. They act as portals for possibility. For example, the altar I build at the beginning of a project is a way for me to thank my muses, and maybe, if they're passing by in spirit and have an offering for me in return, they'll leave me a synchronicity in my daily life as a little bit of extra magic, the first line of a poem, the inspiration for an essay, the concluding paragraph of a story. The best part about magic, at least the magic I do, is that it's experimental, open to mystery, and helps us identify and create our belief systems. There is so much we don't know. *And isn't that freeing?*

This book will walk you through the creation of an elemental writing altar, one that honors the elements and weaves in aspects of your creative practice. After we do this together, you'll be able to craft an altar as an ode to your creativity, to make real a project in the world that's currently living solely as an idea. The possibilities will spiral out and unfold.

Some of my altars are more visible to passersby. They exist in the center of my home, where visitors and friends who come to my apartment can see them (or if you come to class with me via the internet through our video portals). I leave items that belonged to my grandparents resting under the watchful eye of a lace doily made by an ancestor in Poland, framed by my husband in a circular cedar frame.

This altar is intended to memorialize those who came before me in a way that allows me to interact with them daily. I can leave PBR in a glass for my Grandpa Ken and cigarettes for my Grandma Joan. It is an active, remembering altar, built with gratitude in the hopes that one day I will be remembered the same way.

Altars can be bridges between generations, sharing with us the stories of our ancestors.

Other altars are more secretive, existing on desks or in dresser drawers, a collection of knickknacks to the untrained eye. The intention of a desk altar might be to inspire creativity, bring calm during a hectic workday, or signal the beginning of a new client relationship or creative project. An altar built on a dresser or vanity honoring the goddess Aphrodite may look like roses, a row of lipsticks, perfumes, oils, and a seashell.

Altars can also be built in collaboration with the earth. This might look like a stone and some dried herbs left at the base of a tree, or a few acorns and a mandala of leaves placed on the edge of a river. The intention behind one of these altars might be to deepen a connection with the earth and say hello to the spirits that inhabit these spaces.

Some altars are built in collaboration with others. During my MFA program at Sarah Lawrence College, poet and professor Aracelis Girmay instructed us to develop interactive poetry prompts.[1] I brought in items from my home altar and wrote a line of poetry to accompany each item. I then asked my fellow students to write lines of poetry in response to my lines.

Together, we built a single altar of poetry and a physical altar. As I read each line, my classmates stood at the front of the room, read their lines in response, and placed their item on an altar we crafted together in the classroom window. Six years later, this project was in part the inspiration for this book. I saw then how language built an altar when a poem was written together. I saw how as we read and placed the items, the energy and the magic in the room felt tidal, and it created a circle of connection and magic for us.

What You Bring to the Altar

You bring your magic, creativity, and perspective on the world to the altar. This is uniquely you, and it is a gift. Something I cannot say enough is that your intuition (not anxiety, not fear) knows you best. That inner voice you listen to works with writing as a tool, allowing your voice to shine through. You are both unlike anyone else *and* like everyone else, uniquely your own and yet also a part of a community. ***This is magic.***

Throughout the journey you are about to embark on in this book, what you bring to the altar will be symbolic actions, the elements, offerings, your creative lineage, intentions, cycles, and sometimes nothing but yourself (which is always enough).

Word Witches know that your wholeness is inherent.

Remember: there is no way to be "correct" when creating a creative life. As you practice listening to that voice and continually showing up to your practice, you'll feel more supported by what is genuine and authentic to you. In the words of Ms. Frizzle, my patron saint of the creative spirit and the iconic schoolteacher from the children's cartoon series *The Magic School Bus*, "Take chances, make mistakes, get messy!"[2] For the Word Witch, both creating a physical altar and developing a relationship with the page as an altar are powerful places to begin this journey.

Making an Altar for Your Writing Practice

For the writer and the Word Witch, the page itself is an altar. It's where you can bring your creative intentions and focus. You can balance your sentences, adjust your grammar, select your font, or use your handwriting. You can channel all your ideas onto the page, making the intangible tangible, building worlds with your words. By returning to the page day after day, Word Witches cultivate a deeper relationship with this portal of creativity and this practice.

The Word Witch writes in ceremony.

Word Witches can also make altars as physical representations of their writing practice to help support them in their creative journeys. As above, so below. What is created in the physical world works in the etheric realm as well. By creating a dedicated space in your home for writing and deepening your magical practice, you'll find that your pen will channel new words and ways of being.

In each chapter of this book, you'll be guided to add something to an altar dedicated to your writing practice. Through the building blocks of creating an altar, paired with the writing practices, you'll be able to develop your unique practice as a Word Witch. It's my hope, intention, wish, and dream that by the end of this guide, you'll have a deeper relationship with both the craft *and* the craft. There will be a space in your home that is sacred, just for you, one that is devoted to who you are as a writer, human, artist, and Witch. And there will also be a notebook full of rituals, commitments, spells, blessings, and dreams.

All of these altars are woven together.

Their center point is you.

Building an altar is an active practice, as is building a writing practice. You don't have to wait for inspiration to build one; sometimes you don't know how the creative act or impulse will manifest itself until you've begun to carve out space for it.

One of the most important things you can do for your writing practice is to start.

Once you start, you'll begin to see altars everywhere. You are probably already a gifted and talented altar builder, perhaps without knowing it. Think of how you decorated your home! A bookshelf can be an altar. Each book you add to the shelves brings a different energy to the space, a different world, and a different portal of possibility. A desk can be another kind of altar, a flat space where you channel, create, and place photos, statues, and talismans that conjure up memories. A garden can be yet another altar. It's a place, a mantle in the earth that you tend to, that you focus your energy toward, that you cultivate, and from where flowers, herbs, and vegetables grow.

However you start to build your altar, it will become an essential component of your practice as a Word Witch.

Symbolic Action and Correspondences

When you add something to your Word Witch altar, you make associations between sacred objects, artifacts, and their magical potential or what they can mean and represent in your practice. For example, cypress is often associated with the goddess Artemis because it was said that she helped her mother, Leto, deliver her twin brother Apollo while in a cypress grove on the island of Delos.[3] When you add a representation of a specific deity to your altar, you draw in that deity and make a connection in the physical realm.

Symbols are an essential part of storytelling. They are also an important part of altar making. Therefore, it's no mystery that a Word Witch must nurture a deep relationship with symbol and meaning. You don't have to accept preexisting ones, either; you can construct symbols based on your experiences. For example, an oak traditionally symbolizes strength. To me, because of my relationship with oak, it also symbolizes family. You can study a symbol and then consider how it makes you feel and what it reminds you of. Because symbols represent specific things, the more precise you are about what meaning your objects carry and the more accurate they are, the more likely your altar is to channel supportive energy.

In her beautiful publication *Mystery Cult,* author and Witch Amanda Yates Garcia writes about correspondences, saying, "When you work with the correspondences, you draw the essence of the energy you're calling towards you. The correspondence behaves in the same way as the thing it corresponds to because it IS the thing it corresponds to. In the same way that your hair is 'you' even when it is also carbon, oxygen, nitrogen, protein, etc.... Correspondences are at the essence of what magic is all about: resonance and relationship. Magic and witchcraft are based in a mythopoetic ontology (world view). Developing your craft as a Witch means honoring the way that the web of life connects with itself."[4]

Resonance and relationship work in altar building to create symbolic action and correspondence, but also in writing. Words are symbols. Consider how the words carry a vibration when they're placed next to other words. It's magic that when they're put together, they create words and then sentences, aspects of our daily life that we're so accustomed to, but when attempting to explain them, the usual language falls short. By typing an e-l-e-p-h-a-n-t you can see an elephant; it draws the image of the elephant toward us through the page. But it is not actually an elephant. In the same way the symbols create the stories, the symbols craft the altar.

·•☽ Intentions ☾•·

Intentions are discussed in many practices of magic, spirituality, or even mindfulness, and this book is no exception.

Setting an intention is a powerful magic you can make with language. An intention specifies what you want to happen but states it as if it has already happened. Ideally, it is as clear and concise as possible since it communicates what you want and what your desired outcome is. I always try to write my intentions in a single sentence. An example of an intention might be: "I feel ease in my creative writing practice," or "I complete my first novel in the next year and feel proud of my work."

When we know what we're seeking, intentions are easier to track and pay attention to. It can also be helpful to add a time frame to our intentions so we know how to best reflect on our progress. That's why working with the moon is a powerful way to track them. The moon gives energy to our words and a tidal approach to reflection on the process.

It's powerful to feel into these intentions, to see them as something actualized, and then, maybe most importantly, to take the steps to actually make them happen. If you don't write your novel, you won't complete it in the next year and feel proud. But if you set your intentions and do the work required to see it through, magic will work with you.

Sometimes our intentions don't come true or unfold as we expect them to. *This is true of both life and magic.* Remember that it is part of the cocreative process (with the universe or whatever higher power you believe in), one that requires your surrender and trust.

Setting intentions takes time; you must hone and whittle and craft them. As you practice these forthcoming rituals and spells and work seasonally with your writing practice, you'll learn to better understand your intentions and how to craft them most powerfully.

Chapter Three

THE FOUNDATION

When you think of the word "foundation," what images and associations come to mind? Do you think of a house or structure, maybe where you sit and read this book? Do you think of the pillars of a bridge that plunge deep into the waters below? Do you think about the different kinds of root systems that anchor themselves intuitively into the earth to allow trees to grow ancient and wise? Do you think about what it means to build something, to craft something, to care for something, to give it the structure of safety and security?

To me, a foundation allows something to be built upon it with intention. When a proper foundation is laid, then the rest of the "thing," for lack of a better term, can grow from that place. That's why it makes sense for us to start here on your Word Witch journey.

What is your foundation as a writer?

And what will you choose as the foundation for your creative altar?

In the physical sense, this foundation is the place where we assemble our altar, the first item placed. In the creative sense, this foundation can include the physical tools that we use in our writing practices as well as our intentions and commitments to our craft. The foundation or where you build from as a writer is both metaphorical and very real; there are tangible aspects, and there are also hopes, dreams, intentions, and the more etheric perspective of the metaphorical roots.

First let's discuss the inspiration for what the foundation of a physical altar can be. Then we'll dive into what the foundation of your writing practice with your Word Witch journal will look like.

The Physical Foundation

Every altar has a foundation. The makings of this foundation, though, may vary—an altar table built with your hands, the dirt of the earth, the roots of a tree, the mantel in your studio apartment, the fireplace in your home, the windowsill of a dorm room, a shelf you've fastened into the wall, a silk scarf, a scrap of cloth are all possibilities. Think of the foundation of your altar much like the foundation of a house: It structures and supports, it allows the house to be grounded in something, it creates stability, and it provides a base for what we might call home.

Some altars are movable and can be taken with us wherever we roam. This means we might have to get a little creative with their physical foundations, perhaps tucking our sacred items into a bandana, box, or handkerchief. This can be an excellent way to travel with magic in your back pocket and create a sacred space wherever we go.

The foundation of one altar I will never forget is an altar that my husband, Cody, and I were fortunate to visit in Antiparos, Greece. After we got engaged, we went to Greece and traveled to Paros by ferry, rented a scooter, and took a second ferry out to an island where there was a neolithic cave that was once a worship place for the goddess Artemis.

An eighteenth-century church called the Church of Agios Ioannis Spiliotis (Saint John of the Cave) now watches over the entrance to the cave.[1] As we descended the stairs into the belly of the cave, we could feel the air change, like a different climate, one crafted from ancientness. On our map, we saw a stone tucked behind larger stones in an adjoining chamber labeled "altar." We ducked behind the stones and put our hands against the cool rock, and though there were no offerings, altar cloths, or candles there, we immediately recognized the sacred foundation of the place. The stone kept its secrets, memories, and rituals, but we could still feel it in our palms, the cool rock, the spirits of the cave whispering, and the idea that we were part of a long tradition of humans participating in this.

Pause now and look around your space. What foundations do you see? If you're outside, put your palms flat against the dirt or grass. Notice where your feet connect or where your bones feel into the earth. A foundation can be anywhere, from the place where a glass of water meets your desk, the wooden floor of your space, the couch, the bed, or the points where the mattress meets the bed frame or the fireplace holds a fire.

Ultimately, the foundation is a meeting point, a space of connection, a place of rest. The earth itself has a mantle—its earthiness, that which compacts down to the core—that we as living beings rest upon. It is where we grow from.

✸ *The Word Witch puts their roots down and listens.* ✸

Consider what you'd like to be the foundation of the physical altar you're crafting in your space. Perhaps you'd like to use a windowsill, a box that can be tucked away, a table, a bookshelf, or a desk. This space will be sacred to you while you follow the prompts and practice the rituals of this book.

So, spend some time thinking about what cultivating a space of creativity looks like for you. If you have an office where you like to write, go there. If you prefer spending time on the porch writing with your dog at your feet, build your altar there. If you enjoy climbing out of a window to sit on a fire escape and let the sounds of the city inspire you, excellent. Or, if you favor writing outside of your house in a park or a coffee shop, consider making your altar portable.

The word "sacred" comes from the old French *sacrer,* meaning to "consecrate, anoint, dedicate." Wherever you choose to place your altar, it will be consecrated as a physical dedication representing your creative process. It should be somewhere where you feel inspired, where you are able to be yourself, where you can spend time calling and culling and crafting.

This book was written at a desk with a desk altar, an ancestral altar, and my oak tree waving from the window. It was also written from my couch while I scratched my dog's head, with a window altar nearby. These are my sacred spaces.

·•☽ Sacred Spaces ☾•·

A sacred space is anywhere you deem sacred; it is where your altar will rest. While aesthetics can help create this energy, the most important thing is how the space feels to *you*. As an example, I often think about the landscape where Georgia O'Keeffe painted while living at Ghost Ranch in New Mexico. Though I never made it to her home, I drove the highways outside of Taos, inspired myself by the stones, the sky, the spirit of the land there. She first visited in 1934, staying for a summer in one of the cottages. In 1940, she became the owner of a house on seven acres of the ranch, which inspired her work.[2] This landscape, immortalized in her creations, has inspired many others, before and after her. About her sacred space she said, "Out here, half your work is done for you."[3]

The space where you write is a part of your foundation. My apartment in Brooklyn is one of these spaces, with its quiet backyard, my office facing the street, an oak tree, a brick wall, and kind neighbors. I have been creating in this space for the last eight years. It came to me in a strange almost fated way, adding to the lore of the place. (It wasn't for rent; I was there to see the next-door apartment with no outdoor access; I bonded with the landlord over Polish ancestry; when I opened the refrigerator there was only a beer from the small-town brewery in Michigan where I went to college. I asked for the lease immediately.) It has informed my work in new ways, and I am constantly inspired by my surroundings.

There are many kinds of sacred spaces. A desk can be holy, a bed can be holy, and your office can be holy. In my childhood bedroom, I wrote at the desk that belonged previously to my mom's grandma, Ella, which was filled with ancestral magic. I know Witches who write in greenhouses and gardens, in converted closets with desks, on park benches. If you deem it sacred, then it's sacred.

Beyond crafting a dedicated altar, there are a few ways to "make holy" a space for your writing. Consider the colors you paint your walls, the pictures you decorate with, the scents you call upon. Take Casa Azul, the home of Frida Kahlo in Mexico City, which is the most inspiring and potent shade of blue I have ever seen. Of course, the sacredness of that space inspired in part the famous painter to create her masterpieces.

Once the space is designated, you can add whatever you like to it. Whenever I'm working on a big project, for example, I make sure to have fresh flowers in my home because they remind me to write with creativity, kindness, and love for the world. The materials in your space can and should be intentional. My husband crafted my desk chair out of white oak and walnut for me, and I feel the grounding nature of the trees as I teach from my desk. I keep my ancestral altar behind my desk to feel my ancestors always at my back, urging me forward.

Make your Word Witch space sacred to you. If for any reason, you cannot physically alter the space itself, consider changing your appearance in your space. You might have a hair pick you always tuck into your hair while working; you might paint your fingernails blue to better channel your next book; you might wear a scarf that reminds you to write, write, write.

You can be your sacred space.

Just decide it and it's so.

•◗ The Foundation of Your Altar ◖•

Next, decide if you'd like to add anything to the foundation to create the base for your altar. You can use an altar cloth, a silk scarf that was your grandmother's, or a piece of fabric you found at Goodwill that makes you smile. You can dye cloth with ritual plants (I once used acorns to dye silk a beautiful gray-purple color) or use a board of wood, bringing into your practice the energy of your favorite tree. You must designate the base of your altar from which you'll build.

The altar we're crafting together specifically supports your writing practice and your life as a Word Witch, so consider what that means to you. Is there a way through symbolism to build an altar "in the real world" that better mirrors the altar in your writing practice?

When you have selected your foundation, I'd like you to say a blessing of beginning. Whether you have chosen the roots of a beloved tree outside in your neighborhood, a small closeable box, your fireplace, or your windowsill, put your palms against the surface and say aloud:

With this foundation,
I build a space to thrive,

an altar space to come to life,
and through this space,
for the highest good I make,
this foundation for
my inner Word Witch's sake.

This space is now ready for you to begin your process. It begins in ritual.

·•☽ The Importance of Ritual ☾•·

Word Witches know that rituals allow us to be actively present and participatory in our lives, in collaboration with the universe and the divine.

Rituals were born into this world through caverns, carvings, petroglyphs, songs and dances, and oral traditions. The word "ritual" comes from the etymology of ceremony or performing religious rites, but this word is an innate part of being human and from and of this earth. Rituals are ways to celebrate, mourn, grieve, and honor the human experience; they are a dance that we perform together. A ritual is "an act or series of acts regularly repeated in a set precise manner."[4]

In 2006, archaeologists in the Kalahari Desert of Botswana found the site of what is believed to be one of the earliest discovered human rituals, from seventy thousand years ago. There they found a stone snake, approximately six feet tall and twenty feet long. This snake, discovered by nearby carved arrowheads (though there were no other tools or signs of habitation), would have, in the firelight of this ritual, appeared to move, dance, and shimmer in the night, illuminated by the flames.

In this ancient and remote area in Tsodilo Hills, known to the modern San people as "Mountains of the Gods," their mythology states that humans came from a deified python, a creature who created the surrounding earth, an origin story, making this discovered ritual even more powerful, a link between today and the mysterious past. The snake wove its way into the stories, there at the earliest rituals.[5]

Rituals help us make sense of the world around us and embrace its mystery. They remind us that the unknown is fertile and fecund ground for meeting ourselves, the gods, and all that is divine. Rituals allow us to sing together in the hollow of a forest, gather by a stream to speak oaths, burn a fire, and give offerings.

Rituals allow us to meet both the challenge and the magic of the world head-on. Through ritual, we can embody the strange beauty of our lives. Rituals allow us to face the unknown and the uncertain. Ritual is a series of actions, yes, but ritual is also a dance.

A ritual can help us in our creative practice by giving us the space and support to feel our most creative and authentic selves present and allow this voice to speak. Creating rituals, or writuals (writing rituals), is an act of experimentation and play. It is a way to access the magic and the language of being alive. Rituals mark time, they honor, they conjure, and they create. Through ritual, magic is possible.

Magical Foundation: Introduction to the Elements

Beyond the foundation of our altar in our space and the underlying importance of ritual, the magical elements are the foundation from which we will craft a sacred circle and spiral through the practices in this book.

Science tells us that many elements make up the world around us. And this is true. The periodic table of the elements always fascinated me as a young person, all the building blocks of the world around us. The altar of the world that we live in is intricate, ancient, and beautiful.

From a more alchemical or magical perspective, five elements are the basis of a magical practice: air, fire, water, earth, and spirit. Different iterations of this can be found across Chinese, Japanese, Buddhist, Greek, Babylonian, and European alchemy (and probably more!). The philosophies and cosmologies of these different cultures are vast, and they're all connected to different stories, histories, deities, religions, and perspectives on health and the body, which ripple out across history and time.[6]

In my practice, I work with these elements to create and seek balance and to stay connected and in tune with our planet.

In *Astrology, Psychology, and the Four Elements,* author, psychologist, and astrologer Stephen Arroyo, MA, explains that "the four elements are not merely 'symbols' or abstract concepts, but rather . . . they refer to the vital forces that make up the entire creation that can be perceived by the physical senses. (This is why the zodiac was referred to in ancient times as the 'soul of nature.') The elements are therefore not only the foundation of astrology and all occult sciences, but they comprise everything we can normally perceive and experience."[7]

In simple terms, the elements are the building blocks of a magical practice. They are associated with astrological signs and directions and are connected to symbolic action, yes, but they're also the vital life force behind this work. We can call on the elements to support our connection to the planet magically and, in turn, deepen our relationship to magic and our creativity. It's all connected.

Many Witches work with these elements when building their altars. In my apprenticeship, I learned to work with the elements by calling a circle. (More on creating an energetic container or calling a circle later.) To do so, I celebrate, honor, and call out to the air in the east, the fire in the south, the water in the west, and the earth in the north, the below, the above, and the center. However, there are many ways to honor the elements, depending on where you are in the world and what lineage you've been taught.[8]

The items we put on an altar to work with the associations of the elements make the elements visible, real, and tangible in our homes. In this book, I've aligned different practices in a writing life with different elements. Together you'll create an altar with the support of the elements, and a writing life, with your words and these practices. Word Witchery made real in the world.

The Elements and the Word Witch

After the foundation, the chapters in this book are devoted to the elements in the order I call a circle. They weave in ideas for the Word

Witch to draw upon these items for your altar of creativity but also as allies in your journey as a writer. Working with these elements can help you as a writer know *when* to dive into writing, *when* to connect with the innate fire of a creative practice, *how* to seek flow, *how* to remain grounded and connected, and *why* to keep writing.

If an element calls out to you, give it your time and energy. If you find yourself resisting an element, go there and investigate it.

These elements are teachers, they are archetypes, and they are old stories.

Let them guide your pen.

·•☽ My Associations and Practices ☾•·

Here are some ways that I work with these elements symbolically, on my altars, and in my rituals. I have included the astrological associations, because all of us were born under specific star signs, and this can be a way to relate to the elements in your personal life, though not necessary.

Air

Feathers, incense, a writing utensil, an image of a bird

Air is associated with the east. The sun rises in the east, and because of this, air is associated with new beginnings and the horizon. Air is the energy of our thoughts and ideas. Much like air-associated Mercury, air is mercurial, constantly changing. Whenever we're writing, crafting poetry, or sharing ideas, air energy is being invoked. If you're building an altar, consider including the imagery of a feather, a horizon, or perhaps a writing utensil. In the language of astrology, air is associated with the signs of Gemini, Libra, and Aquarius. To feel the presence of the element of air in your everyday life, all you need to do is step outside, plant your feet firmly in the earth, cast your face up toward the sun, and take a deep breath in, thanking the air for breath and the life it brings.

Fire

△ *Candles, the color red, the image of the phoenix, red crystals or stones*

Fire is associated with the south. Fire magic is the energy of passion and desire. Fire is a driving force, a lit match, and a literal fire in your magical practice. Fire is transformation magic; it's the energy of the phoenix, ashes waiting to be crafted again. Whenever we feel connected to creativity, play, and inspiration, we're working with the element of fire in our creative practice. To work with fire magic, you can burn intentions, call on fire to support release during ritual, and select red crystals for your practice. In the language of astrology, fire is associated with the signs of Aries, Leo, and Sagittarius. To connect with fire in your everyday life, light a red candle, create a bonfire, tend a fire in your fireplace, or keep a red stone in your pocket.

Water

🜄 *A goblet, a chalice, a bowl of water, blue stones, river rocks*

Water is associated with the west. Water magic is the energy of deep emotion and dreams. Water is the setting sun, as the horizon in the west is where the sun sets each night. Water can teach us how to find the flow in our life, to work with the tides and the rain cycles and the lessons of the moon. Whenever we feel in tune with our intuition, paying attention to our creative cycles, or working with the seasons, we're connecting with the cyclical energy of water. In the language of astrology, water is associated with the signs of Cancer, Scorpio, and Pisces.

You can connect with water in your everyday life by spending some time near an ocean, river, or lake; watching the rain fall; placing a vessel of water outside under a full moon; or speaking kind words or blessings into a glass of water before you take a drink.

Earth

Soil, bones, a leaf, a flower, a rock, a crystal

Earth is associated with the north. Earth magic is the energy of being grounded and of Mother Earth herself. Earth is the guardian and elder trees, oak, pine, and cedar (to name a few). Earth is the more-than-human kin, deer, fox, bear, and wolf (to name a few). Earth is the dirt under your fingernails and a feeling of connection on our planet. Call on the element of earth in your magical practice if you feel lost or scattered. Earth supports each step we take. In the language of astrology, earth is associated with the signs of Taurus, Virgo, and Capricorn.

You can connect with earth in your everyday life by tending a houseplant, keeping a garden, going for a walk, or leaning against a tree, saying hello.

Spirit

The liminal, ancestors, the sacred bones, the altar itself

Spirit is associated with the below, the above, and the center. Spirit is the ancestors, the threshold, the liminal, and divine guidance. Working with spirit is working with the mysteries of the world and the forces we cannot see. Spirit magic is the magic of the cosmos, the underworld, celestial beings, and the liminal. The energy and magic of spirit reside within our very soul, connecting us to all that is, has been, and ever will be. When you're connected with spirit, you're in a relationship with the mysteries and unknown of the creative practice. To connect with spirit in your everyday life, you can craft an altar to commune with this space.

·•☽ Calling a Circle ☾•·

Calling a circle invokes and honors the elements of air, fire, water, earth, and spirit. This is done at the beginning of a ritual or before casting a spell and then opened again at the end of the ceremony. The circle is important because it denotes a sacred space and helps focus and share intent. The circle is a potent symbol in witchcraft and magic. It is universal, representing eternity, cyclical movement, and the divine. It has no end but continues to turn into itself. Circles can be created in many ways. You might remember the circle of brooms in the movie *Practical Magic*; salt, crushed eggshells, and flour are other popular choices (never use salt outside, *please*).

✸ *The Word Witch uses language to create a sacred circle.* ✸

During my apprenticeship with Robin Rose Bennett, I learned to create this space by calling to the air in the east, fire in the south, water in the west, earth in the north, the below, the above, and the center, and this practice has rippled out into my practice of writing and magic making.

Calling a circle builds a container that connects us to all that is, creating a spiral of energy and magic to support our work, practice, process, and intentions. It acknowledges all the forces of our planet and all the magic that flows through us and the world around us. Everything is connected in the world of the Word Witch.

Calling a circle before a ritual or spell can help support your words. It's a way to thank the guides, connect with the land you're on, or bring a group's energy together.

To practically call the circle, you stand, if possible, in a circle if you're with others. As you invoke each direction, you turn in a circle, facing each direction, putting your palms up or out to the direction. If you're alone, you can read or speak each part. If you're in a group, you might consider taking turns speaking to the directions individually, while collectively saying "blessed be" after each part.

As you speak to each direction, name the aspects and spirits of this direction. Though I've included my associations above to get you started, it's important to consider what these elements mean to you, especially in your writing practice. When do you feel the shift of the winds with your pen? When do you feel the flow of water in your poetry? The most important part of this practice is your presence and attention. It doesn't need to be long or elaborate (though it can be!). It just needs to originate from your heart.

I've included an example of this circle calling below, but it's important to note that once you establish your relationship with the elements, you won't need a script, and your words can change every time you call the circle. I always try to tailor my circle to the practice I'm about to embark on, to allow the words and elements to know why I'm calling upon them in this specific instance. It also takes practice. If it feels strange at first, that's okay. *It's a practice, and it's for you.* This is really what it means to build your unique relationship with these energies that create our world.

As you speak each part, imagine all the aspects that each element represents and symbolizes for you:

I will now call a circle. Its intention is to create
a magical space, a sacred space,
holding us together here in ritual...

Thank you to the spirits of the air in the east,
air who guides our pens, who gifts us quick winds of
inspiration, air who teaches us about new beginnings and
the rising sun. Air, thank you for our feathered friends
and the cooling breeze. Air, thank you for
your presence here in our circle. Blessed be.

Thank you to the spirits of the fire in the south,
fire who knows our inner desires and passions, who offers
a lit candle, the spark of the match of creativity. Fire,
thank you for reminding us the importance of shadows,

play, and dance. Thank you for your
presence here in our circle. Blessed be.

Thank you to the spirits of the water in the west,
water who teaches us divine flow, who is cyclical magic,
the tides, the moon. Water, thank you for teaching us the
old stories, for grandmother energy,
for our emotions, and for our dreams. Thank you for your
presence here in our circle. Blessed be.

Thank you to the spirits of the earth in the north,
earth who teaches us to be grounded, who is our
more-than-human kin, fox, bear, deer, who knows the
guardian trees, oak, cedar, pine. Earth, thank you for
teaching us the messages of the roots and helping us to
stay connected. Thank you for your presence
here in our circle. Blessed be.

Thank you to the spirits of the below, below who holds
the sacred bones of the ancestors, of the holy soil, below,
who knows the old, old stories. Thank you to the below for
holding us here in our circle. Thank you for your presence
here in our circle. Blessed be.

Thank you to the spirits of the above, above who are
the constellations, the stories of the stars, all the lessons
of the cosmos. Above, thank you for reminding us that we
spin together in our circle,

here in space. Thank you for your presence
here in our circle. Blessed be.

Thank you to the spirit of the center, the center
from which our circle spirals and spokes and turns.
The center who teaches us divine understanding
and love. Thank you for your presence here
in our circle. Blessed be.

Our circle is cast; we are between worlds.

When your spell or ritual is complete, open the energetic circle by calling the directions in reverse, turning in a reverse motion, and giving thanks for their presence during your practice. Robin taught us to open our circle by saying or singing, *"May the peace of the Goddess live forever in our hearts. Our circle is open, yet unbroken, merry meet, and merry part, merry meet, and merry part, merry meet, and merry part and merry meet again."*

The Foundation of Your Writing Practice

The first thing you'll need for your writing practice is a journal to document your rituals and processes as you move through the prompts and writing exercises in this guide. Choosing a journal is a personal process. I always use the same softcover journal—in black, with no lines—because I like to let my words find themselves as they sing all over the place. Others might prefer thin or thick margins, grids or ruler marks, colorful patterns and borders.

Consider a journal you feel in partnership with and not one that feels intimidating or too "fancy." The journal *can* be beautiful and elegant and decorative, of course—as long as you're willing to write in it. The journal can also exist beyond what we consider a standard journal to look like. It can be a laptop if typing is more accessible to you. It can be voice memos if speaking aloud is a better way for you to process your thoughts. I know Word Witches who consider a typewriter a must. (Just look at Joan Didion's famous packing list![9]) Decide what a journal means for your practice, and then dedicate yourself to the relationship with this object.

✸ *Word Witches make illuminating mistakes*
and conjure up beautiful drafts within its pages. ✸

Before you begin this new Word Witch journal, I'd invite you to consecrate your physical foundation for this practice.

It's time to begin.

First become grounded in front of your journal and find stillness, holding the journal in your hands or letting it rest on your lap. If you'd like, you can do this next to the foundation you've created for your Word Witch altar. Take three deep, clearing breaths: in and out, in and out, in and out.

Then affirm your intentions out loud:

This journal is a tool to aid me in my spiritual development;
it is consecrated to be of service to myself, my magic,
and anyone I come into contact with who is
open to receiving its gifts.

Next you can recite this spell:

This sacred object here with me
in my magical practice is a key.
This tool is sacred, intention real,
and with this spell, I give my seal.

Afterward, you may finish your spell with "blessed be," "so mote it be," or "so mote it be or something better." Kristin Lisenby and I always say "So mote it be or something better" at the end of our spells to be open to whatever the universe, divine timing, and the powers that be have in store for us, because we know that we don't always know. The mystery is part of the fun of magic. Choose whatever language resonates with your practice. Then, use the tool immediately to bind the consecration.

✸ *If you're asking what you should write, don't worry.*
This Word Witch has something in mind for you. ✸

Ritual:
·•☽ A Cord-Cutting Release Ritual ☾•·

You are probably arriving at this practice with at least one preconceived notion about being a writer or a Witch. One thing I can promise you is that these definitions are always going to change for you. Identities are constantly in flux. They're like tides. The best way to surf these waves is to stay true to your vision and your work in the world. The best way is to have a clear and intentional practice of how you see your work. This vision can be blocked by all the noise and preconceived notions that exist in the space. There's a chance that this preconceived notion is holding you back. For example, this might be "I'm not really a writer," or "I have nothing to say." The list can go on and on.

I'd like you to take a piece of paper, separate from your Word Witch journal, and write down as many preconceived notions about yourself, writing, and witchcraft you have that you're ready to release. If you're not prepared to let go of them yet, don't write them down. You can always repeat this ritual as necessary. As you write them, imagine these thoughts moving away from you. Then I'd like you to write in your Word Witch journal, and for every thought you release, write an idea to replace it with a positive affirmation. So, if you think "I'm not a writer," your affirming statement for your journal is "I'm a writer."

The next time you feel the past thoughts creeping in, you can turn to this notion that you're setting into motion now at the beginning of this journal. I'd like you to roll or fold the piece of paper you're releasing away from you, and you can shred, burn, or dispose of the thoughts you're releasing. (Always dispose of ritual materials safely with attention to the environment.)

Ritual:
·•☽ Naming and Reclamation ☾•·

Now it's time to practice our Word Witch ritual of naming and reclamation.

When I was a child, in the third grade at Sherman Elementary School, Conrad Hilberry, a Michigan poet, visited our class. At the beginning of our time together, he invited us to take out our notebooks and write our names on the first page. Then he went around and added "is a poet" and then signed his name. I didn't realize then that he'd permitted us to be writers and artists. As an older poet, he knew in his bones that to follow the path of the writer, giving yourself permission is one of the most essential tools in your toolbox. I still have this notebook, an artifact across lifetimes.

Regardless of the name you choose, naming *yourself* is one of the most potent rituals you can practice. You know yourself best—and knowing and honoring yourself is powerful.

For this ritual, imagine a word that feels powerful to reclaim. What do you wish to name yourself creatively? Find somewhere quiet to journal about this, imagining all the energy that belongs to you returning to you and embracing your inherent wholeness.

When you're ready, I invite you to take out your journal, write your name, and add "is a poet," "is a writer," "is a storyteller," or "is a Word Witch"—whatever name or language you wish to give yourself.

✸ *And as you write this, know that this, too, is a spell.* ✸

Ritual: Saying Yes to the Word Witch Path

Saying yes is a powerful spell. After you have written your affirmations about yourself and claimed a name for yourself, we will commit to the Word Witch path together. One of the first books I loved about writing is called *Letters to a Young Poet* by Rainer Maria Rilke. In this book he writes, "In the deepest hour of the night, confess to yourself that you would die if you were forbidden to write. And look deep into your heart where it spreads its roots, the answer, and ask yourself, must I write?"[10] This quote has stayed with me because it's helped me connect to my purpose as a writer. I always knew I needed to write, and so here we are. This can look however it needs to for your practice at this moment.

And if the answer is yes, you must write, or you hear the call of your creativity, then write "yes" in your Word Witch journal.

It can be as straightforward as "Yes, I must write" or as involved as a whole proclamation or manifesto for your creative practice. You can write "yes" in big and bold letters, crossing lines and zigzagging across your page. Be as simple or as ecstatic as you like.

This piece of writing is a living piece of writing. You can return to it whenever you want and continue to weave it into the tapestry of your practice and perspective. The reason you answered "yes" might grow and change over time. Feel inspired to let the path appear under your feet as you travel. You can't know what you don't know, so allow the mystery to do its work.

Allow yourself to feel these intentions deep down in your bones. Know that you are made up of all your ancestors since the beginning of time and stardust. Allow this magic to support your intentions.

✸ *You are a Word Witch, and this is your foundation.* ✸

Journaling Prompts for Your Word Witch Journal

1. What relationship do you currently have with writing? Is writing something you do every day already? Do you feel like a "writer" in your daily life? Is this a word you feel comfortable embracing, celebrating, or singing from the mountaintop?
2. What does the word "foundation" conjure up for you? What about "commitment"?
3. Search online for the writing schedules of famous writers. Which ones speak to you, and why?
4. What feels joyful about writing? What feels challenging about writing? Is there an overlap between the two?
5. Is there any shame or guilt you'd like to release from your identity as a writer?
6. What can you celebrate *right now* about yourself as a writer?
7. How would you like to build your writing life moving forward from this foundation you're currently crafting? Is there a journaling practice you wish to develop? Do you hope to one day write books? Do you long to feel more creative in your everyday life?
8. When did writing as a craft begin calling to you? What secrets might there be in that first initial meeting that can help you develop that relationship?

9. What is one word to describe how you'd like to feel in your writing practice?
10. Can you write about your associations with air, fire, water, earth, and spirit?
11. After you connect with these associations, try writing your own circle to be used before you write.
12. How did you choose your Word Witch journal?
13. What did you discover by moving through the three rituals and consecrating your journal?

Chapter Four

AIR

Working with the Breath for Blessings and Spells

The Air Element

Direction: the east
Symbolic Magic: feathers, wind chimes, incense
Associations: writing and language, sunrise, beginnings, feathered friends, winged creatures
The Ritual: spells, writing a blessing

In the beginning, there was breath—and there was story. Our lives begin with a breath. And so, with our foundation sturdy, we start with the element of air.

Word Witches cast spells with their breath and their

sacred words. In magic and ritual, air is associated with the east, the direction of poetry, writing, words, sunrises, and new beginnings. In this chapter we'll discuss how and why to incorporate air into your Word Witch altar. Then we'll talk about casting spells, and I'll show you how to hold a ritual of writing a blessing.

First take a deep breath. As you breathe in, imagine every first, last, and lifetime of breaths taken by every human, and every more-than-human being, that has ever lived on this earth. Breath keeps us tethered to this planet. It is our connective thread.

Air sustains us. It circles through our lungs in an innately intuitive way, making life possible. When I think about breath, I think of the way a deep breath can calm me down or the way my breath directly feeds the trees as they take my exhalations and nourish themselves.

✸ *This is the cyclical magic of air.* ✸

Breath is a sacred commonality between us and our more-than-human kin. When I think about the impulse to breathe, I think about dolphins. When they're born, the other mothers of the pod can help deliver the baby, and together, as a single unit, they guide the newborn to the surface to take their first breath. Collectively, they honor the experience of this initial breath. They know it as an instinct; it is essential for survival. *This is a poem.* I think about the way I've heard dolphins breathing together through a storm over the ocean. They were a chorus.

Breath connects us to the trees. Forests are called the lungs of the planet, absorbing carbon dioxide that we exhale and then producing life-giving oxygen. We are in a constant dialogue with these guardians, the air that moves their branches as if saying hello. We are not so different from these beings. In his bestselling novel *The Overstory,* Richard Powers writes, "You and the tree in your backyard come from a common ancestor. A billion and a half years ago, the two of you parted ways. But even now, after an immense journey in separate directions, that tree and you still share a quarter of your genes."[1] Beyond our breath, our very DNA weaves into the branches of these air creators. The trees give us the breath that allows for our stories. We are a part of the lungs of the earth.

I also, of course, think of the birds, our feathered friends and great navigators of the air. Someone once told me that if I noticed feathers on the sidewalk, it was a sign that I was walking the right path. Birds speak in the language of synchronicity. They soar on the winds of the seasonal change, filling the morning with burgeoning calls, the hawk outside my window here, even in New York City, the robin that arrives with spring upstate, the red-tailed hawk in the Michigan field.

Birds are wise guardians from the air. In her book *Refuge: An Unnatural History of Family and Place,* Terry Tempest Williams writes, "I pray to the birds because they remind me of what I love rather than what I fear. And at the end of my prayers, they teach me how to listen."[2] The birds teach the writer how to listen.

What birds live near you? What birds share the air with you? When I think of witching birds, I often consider the turkey vulture, for their lessons of death and alchemy.

Turkey vultures are fed from the cycles of life and death and do not end lives but rather alchemize what has already passed and gone. Not only do turkey vultures clean up what is decaying, but they actually clean the air when they take flight with their feathers. Their feathers are often used in cleansing rituals. They are death's companion and are the great caretakers of the balance of things. They fly in a spiral, a wide circle overhead, an oscillating poem about death and grief. The turkey vulture visited with my sister and me before our grandpa passed through the veil, and I'll never forget the strange way in which nature's oracle helped prepare us for what would come. The turkey vulture is a guardian, an attendant, a great teacher of air's magic, because the beginning and endings are always linked.

So, what can this teach us about the creative process? It can teach us that the air is constantly changing. It changes directions, it transforms and it picks up quickly. Air is a blessing.

Another bird that teaches me about writing is the starling. You might see them in the parks if you live in New York City. In McGolrick Park, a park in Greenpoint, I often see them with their midnight bodies and the iridescence of their feathers.

Starlings teach me about the breath and the line on the page. Starlings move in murmuration, clusters that dive and swoop through the air together. Over the field at my grandpa's house, I have seen them at both dawn and dusk creating poetry in the sky. They form lines and line breaks; they are calligraphy, brush stroke, and rhythm. Starlings sing a song of resonance. Studies have found that each starling responds to six or seven of its nearest neighbors to move together; this number balances the cohesion of the group with each individual. They take flight on the same winds, together though separate. On the page, our prose and poems might look like the murmuration of starlings. These words move toward and away from each other. Some pieces are painted in long lines, and others, a single mark.

Guided by the dolphins, trees, turkey vultures, and starlings, consider how air is a vital part of your writing practice. Air is the life force that fills our lungs and allows us to speak our work aloud. Even as air is the beginning, it is always linked to the end because that is the magic of the circle.

·•☽ Air on Your Word Witch Altar ☾•·

In a magical practice, air can be represented by many different items. Feathers are a beautiful way to incorporate air into your altar and connect with these feathered friends. I also think of the way that pine moves in the breeze, with its needles, and have used pine or other air-like plants to symbolize air.

You might consider incense on your altar to represent the air, as the smoke billows when lit.

Another way to represent air is by hanging wind chimes. Whenever there is a breeze or air moves near your altar, you'll be able to hear it.

You can also write a spell or craft a blessing (which we'll do together in a moment). This can be a beautiful way to add the element of air without any additional materials needed.

Whatever you decide, as you place the item on your altar, consider how the breath we breathe, the air we feel, and all that air symbolizes appears in your writing practice. Air represents new beginnings, horizons, poems, and how we communicate and speak. Air is quick. It changes. It knows how to begin again, and it knows how to keep moving. Air is full of winged messengers and muses who guide us as we write.

Think about the new beginnings you'd like to foster or cultivate in your work. Perhaps this is a specific project, like a novel you've been dreaming of, that needs wings to help it take flight. Or maybe it's more of an overall feeling you'd like to call into your work, an energetic new beginning allowing you to relate and come to the page in a new way.

As you place the item on your altar, add it to the east end of the space and speak aloud what the element of air means to you now in your practice as a Word Witch. Thank the spirits of the air for their gifts and presence on your altar.

Ritual:
•☽ Air Magic ☾•

Once you have chosen your symbolic magic for air, I invite you to take out your Word Witch journal and write about your choice. Why have you chosen this object? And what story does it have to share with you? You might think about how air is related to your practice and how, as you selected this item, you felt the symbolic resonance between the two.

To get started, consider reflecting on one or more of these prompts:

1. Why have you chosen this artifact/symbol?
2. How do you see air and the foundation as connected?

3. What does selecting an item intentionally teach you about building an altar?
4. How do you see air related to your creativity and writing?

Air in Your Writing Practice

Breathing comes instinctively, intuitively, and impulsively; this breath is instinct embodied. It allows for speech and communication. We center and ground ourselves through breath, grieve, celebrate, sing, and tell stories. Breath is a unit of being alive, as is the rushing of our blood or the beating of our hearts. As you read this, take three deep breaths with me: *in and out, and in and out, and in and out.*

The breath is both line and white space on the page. The lung of the page rises and falls with us, breathing in sync. There is much writing on the craft of constructing a poem, hammering syllables, and finding the voice through meter and technique. But for the purposes of the Word Witch, today let's get the breath into our bodies and our writing first.

Now I want you to find a piece of writing you love. A poem may be the easiest because of its distinct lines. This can be a poem you've written, a poem you find on your bookshelf or the stacks of the library, or one you find online. (I love the selection on the Poetry Foundation's website.)

Then read this piece aloud to yourself. As you read the poem, notice how your breath expands and contracts, where you take pauses and feel compelled to breathe deeply before tumbling through words quickly, as if possessed. Look for clues in how the words are strung together like beads, where they bump against each other, where the line breaks create a horizon, where the comma instructs you to hold your breath and pause, and where the period rests.

Take time to figure out where the piece lives in your body. Just as some chants can be felt in the belly, some poems can be felt in the back of the throat. I can't read Marie Howe's "What the Living Do" without feeling the grief wash over me, I can't read "Thank You" by Ross Gay without feeling deep gratitude swelling in my chest, and "I—Toward a Definition" by Alice Notley can almost always make me cry, requiring a tiny gasp to get through the poem.

The breath also gives life to language. Translator and poet Paul Celan said it like this: "Poetry is perhaps this: an Atemwende, a turning of our breath. Who knows, perhaps poetry goes its way—the way of art—for the sake of just such a turn?"[3]

"Atemwende" is a word used, conjured by Celan, defined by Edmund de Waal as "the strange moment of pause between breathing in and breathing out, your sense of self is suspended, and you are open to everything."[4] When you breathe in, connect with that pause before breathing out. What can it teach you about your writing or how you express yourself? What might you feel in the body?

Like Waal said, this breath makes you open to everything. The Word Witch opens to everything. Breath expands our lungs, rising and falling, opening to magic and then releasing.

Magic makers know that sometimes we must create a new language. We must breathe our life into our work to make sense of being human.

·•☽ Spell Crafting ☾•·

In my practice, spell crafting is connected to air magic. Spells are starting points. They are seeds. A spell is an invocation, an incantation, or Word Witchery spoken aloud to bring about a change or set an intention with the support of magic. From ancient texts to modern grimoires, spells have been created and used for centuries. Some of the oldest found writing from Egypt, Mesopotamia, Greece, and Rome are spells. They are cuneiform clay tablets and pottery, crafted from magical symbols and language. These unearthed grimoires explain rituals and guide the practitioner in a relationship with mystery and the divine.[5] The proof of spells is as old as language itself, showing the human impulse to create magic for an intended outcome.

Spells can take many forms and can be cast for various reasons: spells of self-love, spells of unblocking paths, spells for healing, and spells for protection. And though many books can offer supportive templates or even spells that you can use in your practice, the most potent spell that exists is the one you create yourself.

A spell spells out an intended desire, outcome, or intention (the mystical connection between spell and spelling!). It's a ritualized statement of a vision. As I travel on my Word Witch path, I find that my spells are about connection, ritual, and thanking the magic that works in my life, always for the highest good of a situation.

To me, spells are about collaborating with the universe and the divine through resonance and symbols. They are about honoring the cycles and patterns of life. My best spells have clarity of intention, a moment where I speak aloud and then embody the magic in my life. The best spells are the ones that are about trusting in how things unfold.

·•☽ How to Cast a Spell ☾•·

Step One: When you sit down to craft a spell, you must first believe in your magical ability and embrace the feeling as if your spell has been fulfilled. Then set your intention as clearly as possible. Consider your "why." Why do you want this spell to be set in motion? What motivation exists under your intention, and why is it important to you? You might spend some time journaling in this phase to better understand your intent and your why.

Step Two: Then, in simple terms, write out the spell. This can come in a rhyme or rhythm or work with a different prose structure. Studying different preexisting kinds of rhymes and meters can support your practice in writing spells, but it is optional.

Step Three: The most essential part of crafting a spell is being sincere and straightforward about your intention unfolding. This can take practice, but that's why Witchcraft has long been called the craft. It is a craft that takes practice, repeatedly returning to your spellwork to refine it over time.

Step Four: Once your spell has been written, prepare your ritual space. You can assist the spell by working with different tools and materials—including the elements, herbs, colors, oils, and candles, among other rituals and practices—to bolster the magic. Also, consider casting a magical circle as a container for the spell, working with the elements, and asking for their support and presence as you enact your ritual. The example of this is in our foundations chapter if you need to return on the spiral path to that point.

Step Five: Speak the spell aloud! This is an excellent way to embody the spell and add power to your written words. Add phrases like "blessed be," "so mote it is," or "so it is" to close your spell. This is like putting a seal on the spell before sending it out into the universe.

Step Six: Once your spell has been cast, you might leave the altar up for a set time (a moon phase is always a potent way to spellcast) or safely discard or put away your ritual items. Always be mindful of your environment.

Step Seven: Gratitude is an essential and final aspect of the spell. Give thanks to the magic and know that the spell will unfold in the way it is ultimately meant to for the highest good.

When I'm writing the spell itself, I find that the process (for me) is swift. I weigh each word, allowing the winds of my intuition to guide my sails. I allow my breath to break the line, knowing that the reading of the spell aloud will add to the magic. When the words meet the air, when I say it with feeling, my spell is cast. The winds carry it up and out to the listening ear of our connected planet.

✸ *The Word Witch trusts that the words will appear on the page.* ✸

If you need a simple rhyme scheme, try this . . .

A
A
B
B

I cast a spell for Witches who write
so, the truth and their stories they might
share and free their pens to cast
a spell of Word Witchery to last

This simple style of spell writing uses two rhyming couplets, or two lines, and stacks two couplets together to create a spell. You can add more lines by adding CC, DD, as desired. Try it out and see how this structure feels for you.

Ritual:
Gratitude and Blessing as a Spell

Your ritual for casting a spell is to write a blessing. Blessings are a kind of spell. They are spells that gift positive energy or invoke spiritual protection and love. Blessings are beautiful ways to express gratitude. Decide on something to which you would like to offer your thanks, breath, and poetic line. This might be a relationship; a pet; the sun, moon, or stars; nourishment; or anything your heart is drawn to.

Once you've decided what you would like to bless with your spell (may I suggest a blessing on your new altar, your writing practice, or both?), you will write to finish the lines I've plotted below. (You'll find more information on the more advanced seven-line writing structure in the section about earth.) Feel empowered to make the prompt your own, using it as a vessel to fill or empty to create your unique piece.

You can do this exercise as many times as you'd like, building a repertoire of blessings for your magical practice. A blessing is a beautiful way to begin any ritual or magical rite. If you're looking for a way to begin a ritual after crafting the foundation of calling a circle, I suggest writing a blessing, one that honors the moon phase, a specific deity, or a season that you're ritualizing.

There is no right way to do this; however you feel called to complete the lines is the perfect spell. To get you started, I've included three examples of my own below (with the intention of showing variety and bending the rules and the lines to match my own breath and voice). Where you see the blank spaces, you will add your own words. It doesn't have to be a single word, but can instead be a fragment written with the intention of finishing the line.

Title: A Blessing On (Insert Here)

Line One: "A blessing on __________________"
Line Two: "May there always be ______________"
Line Three: "Here with my hands ____________"
Line Four: "An offering ____________________"
Line Five: "Thank you _____________________"
Line Six: "For ___________________________"
Line Seven: "I speak this ____________________"

Once you've completed writing your blessing, speak it aloud. You can practice reading it aloud without adding the ritual or intention to it to practice first. When you're ready to "perform" your blessing, imbue it with your intention, add your ritual, and mean it sincerely and with all your heart. Hearing it in your voice and giving it life with your breath is the perfect way to seal the spell. You can always add, "so mote it be," "so mote it be or something better," or "and so it is."

A Blessing on the Waters

A blessing on the waters that pool
even in storm drains. May there always be
rains for your crops, gardens. Here with

my hands, I open them to face the clouds.
I set my hands on the ocean's surface. This
is an offering of my thanks. Thank you,
for your tides, for your cycles, for rain.
I speak these words, a downpour.

A Blessing on the Dogs

A blessing on the dogs. May there always
be companionship, kin. Here with my hands,
I offer you everything. Meaning, my love.
An offering of everything. Thank you for your
watchful ears, for your soft padded feet,
for curling by my own. I speak this softly
as I wake to watch the sunrise with you.

A Blessing on My Family

A blessing on my family. May there
always be togetherness and memories.
Here with my hands, I take a picture.
I make a meal. I sit outside and stare at
the horizon. An offering of connection.
Thank you for my life. For sharing this
life together. I speak this softly, a Michigan wind.

Journaling Prompts for Your Word Witch Journal

1. What symbols in nature remind you of the element of air?
2. What can the birds who live where you live teach you about this element?
3. Is there a new beginning you can feel taking shape in your writing practice?
4. What does a "horizon" mean to you?
5. What is your definition of a spell?
6. How did it feel to read a blessing aloud? What did you notice about your breath?
7. Watch a video of the murmuration of starlings, then sit down and write. Can you write a poem or a piece of writing that is like a murmuration? Where can the words come together or move apart from each other? How can you weave in many voices to sing one single song?
8. Make an offering to the alchemist that is the turkey vulture in your writing. What do you give to the turkey vulture to devour? What has passed on that must be made new? What are you grieving? Leave this for this sacred bird as a part of the cycle. Start the poem or prose with "To the one who circles overhead, I give you…"
9. Write a blessing on your Word Witch practice (your altar, your journal, your writing).

Chapter Five

FIRE

Working with the Imagination and Inspiration

The Fire Element

Direction: the south
Symbolic Magic: a candle, incense, a red stone
Associations: creativity, desire, play, movement, life, transformation, illumination
The Ritual: automatic writing

Word Witches follow the light of their creativity like a lantern through the shadows of the writing process. Creativity is the fire in your writing practice that will encourage you forward, full of passion and play. In magic, fire is often associated with the south, the direction of creativity, fire, transformation, and inspiration. In this chapter, I'll show you how to seek illumination and celebrate your inspirations. We'll talk about the importance of play and movement in ritual.

On your physical altar, you will select a form of illumination to bring light to your sacred space. In your writing practice, you will develop the tools to romance your imagination and the muses and to connect with the practice of automatic writing.

Something is enchanting about the symbol of light. Throughout the ages, it has been used to represent hope, strength, and warmth, and it's also been connected to inspiration. Sometimes inspiration is light embodied as lightning, a flash of inspiration. Sometimes it's a soft glow in a window, a guiding light home. Sometimes it's a flickering star, a reminder of that deep connection to the cosmos.

I do not know where inspiration comes from, and anyone who tells you facts about this is probably grasping at straws (stars). Inspiration is something of caves, dirt, and mystery incarnate. It is ancient, impulse, poetic sensibility, song that has never been written down. In the Lascaux Caves, one of the most ancient representations of human artwork (approximately thirty-two thousand years old), creativity, and storytelling, anthropologists now believe that the ancient people who lived there might have used fire to make the horses gallop, the images move.[1]

Fire is an animating force.

And it lives in balance with the shadows. You can't glow without the darkness. You can't illuminate the story of ancient beings without having the dark present to support the sacred flames.

Fire is also a transformative force. I often think of the species of pine with serotinous cones that wait patiently for a forest fire. They can hang suspended for years, but only when that heat, that alchemizing element, arrives will the resin be melted, opening the cones up and releasing the seeds to be reborn as new pine trees. In addition to these cones, there are seeds of many plants, like the buckthorn family, growing in the California chaparral ecosystem, that need that fire to regrow. Sometimes fire, what we might think of as destruction, is a natural part of the process.[2]

I do not know how to pin inspiration or illumination down, to make it bend to my will, and I don't want to. However, I do know how to beckon my creativity forth, to be in relationship with this nebulous thing that we call the imagination. It is like walking into a dark cave and waiting for that spark. It's like pinecones unfurling open.

Once I was teaching at a retreat in Quintana Roo, Mexico, with Jungian analyst, I Ching interpreter, and author Bobby Klein. During one of our outings, a man named Pluma, a friend of Bobby's who was local to the area, took us off the beaten path and into the jungle to a cenote. Against every impulse in my body, we climbed a ladder down into the dark and swam through the caves, guided only by flashlights. When we came to an opening, he had us all sit in a circle, in ankle-deep water, turn the flashlights off, and sit in the dark together. Then, under the shallow water, he had us turn our flashlights toward the center of our circle, back on, allowing the lights to radiate together.

Light leads us to one another.
Light is a storyteller.

Later that night, I taught a writing workshop on the beach, guided only by candles; the hosts had crafted a serpent made of flame, seeds, and flowers—a symbol for creation.

The origin of light predates stars; inspiration and creativity predate writing. However, now they are intrinsically woven together, careening through space.

When you work with it intentionally while listening to your inner self, fire is the friend and ally of the Word Witch.

✸ *Fire is the way through to the imagination.* ✸

·•☽ Fire on Your Word Witch Altar ☾•·

A candle can be a cornerstone of any ritual or magical practice. It represents the element of fire, but it also represents the air in its smoke, the water in the melted wax, and the earth in the wick. I like to imagine the first candle ever made—a light in a dark night.

We don't know the precise origin of candles, but they have been used for thousands of years. The Egyptians are often credited with the first candles, five thousand years ago, crafted by soaking the cores of reeds in animal fat.[3] Candles are tangible, yet they also represent something outside the physical realm. Candles shed light on all the unknowns in the darkness. They light the way between worlds.

Illumination comes in many forms; it can be a candle or incense or something that represents this idea in another form. Choosing your source of illumination is deeply personal; you might consider the materials, the maker, the color—among other things. So spend some time really thinking about it (or even writing about it). Many makers online sell wonderful candles, or you can run to your local metaphysical store.

Know that there is not only one way to source this for yourself. Listen to your intuition. For example, you might select a candle whose smell reminds you of the cedar trees that grew beside your house growing up, or another candle that is a lovely shade of lilac, in homage to the lilacs you see in your favorite park that always inspire you when they bloom. Select an addition to your altar that sparks your creative fire, one that—upon adding it to your altar—calls on you to create, encouraging you to dig into that unknown place guided only by the light of the flame. Once you have chosen this item, add it to the south-facing part of your altar, continuing to build the spiral, from the air in the east.

Ritual:
Fire Magic

Once you have chosen your illuminating artifact, I invite you to take out your Word Witch journal and write about your choice. Why have you chosen this object? And what story does it have to share with you?

To get started, consider reflecting on one or more of these prompts:

1. Why did you choose this illuminating artifact? What do you notice about it? What does it remind you of?

2. In what ways do you see the air and the fire connect?
3. What does selecting an item intentionally teach you about building an altar?
4. How do you see fire related to your creativity?

·•☽ Baba Yaga and Illumination ☾•·

My grandma used to tell my sister and me an old story about Vasilisa the Brave (or sometimes the Beautiful) or Vasilisa and Baba Yaga. Baba Yaga is a pan-Slavic mythological figure. She is the Witch of the Woods. She rides a mortar, steering it with a pestle through the sky, and lives in a hut with chicken legs that spin and spiral through the forest. The old crone goes by many names, one of them being Baba Yaga Bony Leg, and this leg crafted of bone tells us that Baba Yaga keeps one foot in the land of the living and the other in the dead. She is a liminal being; she is the Witch of the Woods.

The bones are a symbol that we'll come to later in the Spirit section, but Baba Yaga's fire is our source of illumination here because outside of the home of this mythic and knowing woman, the skulls that create her fence are filled with sacred fire. These bones hold the power of fire, illumination, creativity, and transformation. When you go to the house of the crone in the woods, you won't return home again the same. This is one of the gifts of this element.

In this story (or at least in some tellings of this story, for a story always tendrils), a young woman named Vasilisa lives with her father and mother in a cottage in the forest. Before her mother dies, she gives her brave and beautiful daughter a doll and tells her to listen to the doll, to feed the doll and take care of her. So Vasilisa takes the doll with her everywhere. Her father remarries a horrible woman after her mother's death, and she acquires two new stepsisters.

Whenever her father, the merchant, travels for work, Vasilisa is left to face the punishing and harsh nature of her new family. With each twist and turn, the doll guides her. One day her stepmother discovers that their fire has gone out and knows they must relight it to keep warm and survive. She sends Vasilisa into the dark of the wood at night to seek a spark from the fire that glows consistently in the skull lanterns staked outside Baba Yaga's home.

The doll tells her not to be afraid and to go to the house of the Witch. The doll guides her through the dark and murky forest until suddenly Vasilisa sees a horseman. He is entirely adorned in white and riding a white horse, and with his appearance, dawn begins to fill the sky. Then, surprisingly, another horseman appears. This time he is adorned in red and riding a red horse, and the sun starts to rise. She continues on and finally, after a long, long journey, she arrives at the house of Baba Yaga.

The house is as strange as the tales told to the young woman; it stands on chicken legs, with the fence crafted from human bones and crowned with skulls.

Then, to her surprise, another horseman appears, adorned in black and riding a black horse. As he passes, the night descends upon the traveling girl.

As the forest envelops her in night, the skulls begin to glow, and then with a terrible shriek, Baba Yaga appears riding in her mortar. She rides up to the gate and says the magic spell as the storytellers remember it. "*Little Hut, little Hut, stand the way thy mother placed thee, turn thy back to the forest and thy face to me.*" And so the hut turns to her.

Suddenly Baba Yaga stops and inhales deeply. "Do I smell a human? Who are you! Announce yourself."

Vasilisa says to the old crone, "I am Vasilisa, and my stepmother sent me here to ask you for light to keep warm."

Baba Yaga answers, "Ah, yes, I know of this stepmother of yours. Stay with me. If you do your work well, I will give you the light you desire, but if you do not, I will cook and eat you." A threat as old as the crone herself.

As they enter the hut, the old crone tells Vasilisa that she is tired but that tomorrow she will have to complete some tasks for the old woman. She will need to clean the yard, sweep the hut, and cook her supper. Then take the wheat from the storehouse and pick out of it all the black grains and wild peas.

Afraid, Vasilisa turns to her doll, feeding the doll from her supper. The doll advises her to rest, as everything looks better in the morning. When Vasilisa wakes to the presence of the white knight in the yard and Baba Yaga taking off into the morning, she sees that the work has already been completed.

The doll tells her to rest and cook the old woman supper, and so she does. When the Witch returns and finds everything perfect, she is furious but pleased.

She says, "Tomorrow, you must do all the tasks you've done today, but you must also take the seeds from my storehouse and clean them individually." Again, Vasilisa feels despair filling her heart, but the doll comforts her after the woman sleeps, and Vasilisa feeds the doll. And sure enough, in the morning, the doll has ensured everything is completed. Finally, the day passes, and the black knight rides through the yard, and Baba Yaga returns home to find the jobs completed.

The Witch wants to know why Vasilisa never speaks to her during supper, and Vasilisa responds that she does not dare to upset the old woman. Baba Yaga replies, "Well, you may ask a question, but know that every question does not lead to good. What shall you ask me?"

Vasilisa decides to ask her three questions about the men on horseback, one for each of the knights.

Baba Yaga replies that they are her faithful servants, "my white day, my red sun, my dark night." The old crone asks the young woman if she has any more questions for her, but heeding her warning, guided by her intuition, the young woman says no.

In return, Baba Yaga asks Vasilisa how she was able to finish the tasks, and Vasilisa replies that it was because of the blessings of her dead mother.

The crone stands up, shrieks, and commands that the girl leave her hut as "I will not have anyone blessed crossing my threshold." As Vasilisa leaves the gates of the Baba Yaga, the crone grabs one of the skulls with the burning eyes of fire and gives it to the girl. "May you have the joy of this," she commands.

Placing the skull at the end of a stick, Vasilisa runs through the forest. As she returns home, she throws the skull to the hedge, but the skull speaks to her and tells her, "Take me to your stepmother."

As Vasilisa steps across the threshold, she is welcomed by her stepmother and stepsisters for the first time, as the women had not found fire, heat, or nourishment since Vasilisa left. Now in the hands of the stepmother, the skull burns hotter and brighter and turns the merchant's wife and her two wicked daughters into ash.

Come morning, Vasilisa buries the skull in the ground and goes to the village to live. Following the advice of her beloved doll, Vasilisa weaves a beautiful piece of linen so fine that only the tsar himself could wear it. Upon seeing her work and meeting her, the tsar falls madly in love, and he and Vasilisa are married.[4]

In this story, intuition, ancestry, and the benevolent spirits that watch over Vasilisa guide her to the house of the Witch of the Woods. They aid her, and in doing so, they send her home initiated and illuminated, with the power of fire.

In *Women Who Run with the Wolves,* author Dr. Clarissa Pinkola Estés offers her interpretation of the story: "To let things die is the theme at the end of the tale. Vasilisa has learned well. Does she collapse into a fit of high-pitched shrieking as the skull burns into the malicious ones. No. What must die, dies. How does one make such a decision? One knows . . . By the light of the fiery skull, we know."[5]

The fire makes this new life possible; it is an initiation. Vasilisa listens to her intuition. She cares for the doll that her mother gave her. Through this care and attention, the young woman survives her ordeal in the woods. The fire changes everything when she brings it back to her family. We do not go into the woods to meet the old crone, pass her tests, and remain unchanged.

This is the same for our creative endeavors as well. We do not listen to the creative voice that urges us forward, that guides us to tell our stories, and remain the same. A good story makes things different. A good story is a spell of fire. I tell this story to remind you of your power and to bring the fire home.

Word Witches carry the sacred flame
symbolic of their inner knowing.

Movement and Play with Fire

Much like the power of fire in the old, old stories, fire's other magic is its reminder of the importance of play and movement in ritual. When a candle flickers, it reminds us to dance. When the fire glows, memory is recovered. Gaze into a bonfire or candlelight and allow your mind to travel. *What do you remember?* What was once lived returns through the embers.

As we touched on briefly in our introduction to Word Witchery, the imagination is a place of childlike wonder and whimsy.

Play is something that children do very naturally, much like making art or connecting with the earth. Ritual is play. Play is ritual. Creativity is both. Channel a beginner's mind and a playful approach; you might be surprised by what messages you'll uncover.

For a moment, think about the first impulses of your imagination or your creative practice. Did you love to sing as a child? Or dance? In the field and forest just beyond my grandparents' house, my siblings, cousins, friends, and I developed our imaginary worlds, creating great wars and epic quests. I remember donning a princess dress and running through the trees in search of Avalon with my best friend and sister. These landscapes will forever inspire me, even though I haven't visited Avalon for many, many years. This is the gift of the imagination and the gift of fire. It allows us to return to these places and to fingerpaint in our writing.

If you're struggling to access this place of play, I recommend putting on a song you loved when you were young, grabbing your headphones, and dancing around your space. Pairing movement, memory, and joy are powerful ways to access this place of play. Dancing is in its own way a poem.

Author, activist, and Witch Starhawk writes in *The Spiral Dance: A Rebirth of the Ancient Religion of the Great Goddess*, "Witchcraft is fun. It offers us a chance to play, to act silly, to let the inner child come out. Out of foolishness and play, creativity is born."[6] Though rituals can sometimes be solemn in nature, especially when we're doing work that's important and sacred to us, remember that it doesn't have to be one or the other. There is always a place for this playful spirit in the realm of the Word Witch.

Try to remember the first time you believed in magic, and return to that place, and honor that creative spark that was gifted to you as a young human. It's inherent to your nature. This enchantment is yours. It glows like a lantern hung in your heart.

The Importance of Sharing Our Inner Light

This is a spell we create together. I want you to know me, so I shine my soul's lantern here.

FIRE

In the summer of 2020, I was struggling with figuring out exactly who I wanted to be as a writer and the work I wanted to do in the world. I had just finished my MFA the year before and was no longer held by the complicated hands of academia—which might have been part of the source of this tension. I wasn't sure who I was without assignments and without teachers, and I didn't know where I fit in.

In that moment, a friend and fellow Word Witch, Kristin Lisenby, reached out asking me if I had ever considered podcasting before because a friend of hers, Shelby Bundy, had asked her to create a podcast on behalf of her business, Tamed Wild. I hadn't ever considered the idea before, and the thought of speaking my words out loud to an invisible audience terrified me. But there was something about the proposition that drew me in. The opportunity to build community with another Word Witch was a spark. It was an invitation to travel along with her on this path, and through our creativity and imaginations, we could see what this world might have in store for us.

This Word Witch and I talked about how one day, we would look back and remember the first steps we took down this path. Years later, we recognize the power of taking that first step. I told her that I saw the importance of sharing what's close to our hearts because this way others who feel the same way can find us, too.

We have started calling these brave moments of being seen "soul lanterns"; they are the lights that we shine out in a dark harbor to others who might find inspiration and connection through reflecting on our vulnerable truths. Though the murkiness of the creative world can sometimes be intimidating, there is so much joy to be found when you see a light that looks like yours, that cuts through that inky night with the same purpose. This is the power of illumination, too.[7]

In "We Were Made for These Times," an essay that explains the importance of showing and sharing your soul in shadowy times, Dr. Clarissa Pinkola Estés writes, "The light of the soul throws sparks, can send up flares, builds signal fires, causes proper matters to catch fire. To display the lantern of soul in shadowy times like these, to be fierce and to show mercy toward others; both are acts of immense bravery and greatest necessity."[8] This was the inspiration for the term "soul lantern."

The importance of shining your inner light as a Word Witch is a huge responsibility. But it's important that you do it. This is the brave necessity of finding and walking your authentic creative path. If you don't share your heart, your words, your love for writing with the world, how can you ever expect anyone else to see you as the writer you are? When you permit yourself to express yourself creatively, you give others around you the opportunity to do the same. It builds community. This is the kind of illumination that not only brings our ideas forward but also brings us together.

Ritual:
·•☽ Automatic Writing ☾•·

One of my favorite ways to practice Word Witchery is through automatic writing or channeled writing. This practice is also known as *psychography*. Automatic writing is a ritual approach to writing, one that can help you shake off your waking consciousness and tap into a more significant or collective consciousness that you can then channel onto the page. Automatic writing is a form of channeling and divination. It can produce different types of writing: poetry, prose, lyrics, unrelated words, fragments, or even symbols and drawings.

The exact beginnings of automatic writing or spirit writing are obscured by time. However, historians highlight that the practice of "spirit writing" first appeared in China during the Liu Song dynasty between 420 and 479 CE. This form of writing as communication was utilized for communicating with the unseen forces or spirits, and it was considered a popular practice in many traditional Chinese folk religions.

Roughly five hundred years later, planchette writing, called Fuji, evolved in China. In this practice, special tools are used to receive and write messages from spirit realms. Using a planchette—which often takes the form of a funnel of sand held by two people—the written word is used to bridge the spirit world to the material world.[9]

Similar practices can be found in many other cultures, where pendulums and planchettes hovered over an area where symbols were already placed, guiding the seeker toward the symbols the spirits wanted to communicate to this world. If this sounds familiar, it might be because it's also the basis of modern spirit boards, like the Ouija, that are still used today.

Automatic writing is similar in some ways, yet there are a few important differences to explore. For example, there are no symbols from which the spirit picks to communicate with us in the physical world. Instead, there is only a blank area upon which the spirit creates symbols or words using writing materials held by the seeker.

This form of spirit communication saw a rise in use and popularity in the mid-nineteenth into the twentieth centuries across Europe and the United States, particularly in the years following World War I and the influenza pandemic. Many people at the time were experiencing deep grief and loss, so it makes sense they wished to explore communication with the other side. In this practice, the spiritualism and the surrealist movement intersect. Spiritualism is a social, religious set of beliefs that led to the popularity of séances and other forms of spirit contact during this time.[10] Surrealism is a cultural movement that works with the unconscious mind's expression. This movement included popular artists like Salvador Dalí and Leonora Carrington.[11]

André Breton, born in 1896, is widely considered the founder of surrealism[12] and the first person to apply a surrealist lens to automatic writing.[13] In his *Surrealist Manifesto,* published in 1924 he wrote, "Psychic automatism in its pure state, by which one proposes to express—verbally, by means of the written word, or in any other manner—the actual functioning of thought. Dictated by the thought, in the absence of any control exercised by reason, exempt from any aesthetic or moral concern."[14]

After Breton popularized automatic writing, surrealist artists started applying its principles to help inspire their creative pursuits. They would write or draw as quickly as possible to tap into their subconscious mind while shedding the constraints they believed were interfering with their ability to express themselves authentically.

Over the years, many artists have used this practice to help guide their creativity, like David Byrne,[15] Van Morrison,[16] and one of my favorite poets, Lucille Clifton, whose practice began with the Ouija board. She referred to herself as the "two-headed woman," which she would later title her book published in 1980.[17] Clifton began using a spirit board to help her traverse the spirit world while keeping one foot firmly grounded in the physical realm to craft her poetry.[18]

Automatic writing—in all its forms—is popular in witchcraft and magic today, though there is much debate about where these messages originate from. Some believe they come from our unconscious mind or higher self, while others think our guides or spirits send them to us. You'll have to try it out to see what rings true for you! Whatever you do, make sure that you include ritual and intention in your practice; this helps distinguish it from freewriting, a practice of writing in a free-flowing manner, with no set form.

In my practice of Word Witchery, I have done this exercise with hundreds of writers online, in workshops, and at retreats, and what strikes me is the possibility that it breaks open. Through allowing yourself to just write, you limit judgment and expectation, and in solely scrying with the page and in a ritual practice, you discover what can be seen or uncovered from an empty page. I've seen writers create new symbols, draw pictures, defy the line, and weave in words they don't normally use. I've seen writers switch between languages, ask and answer questions they've been trying to solve, or even channel the outline for that novel that has been eluding them. Let yourself be free, Word Witch, and see how your language meets you there, in that wild and roving approach.

✸ *The Word Witch conjures through an empty page.* ✸

Ritual: Automatic Writing for Connecting to Your Inner Creative Spirit

Now I invite you to try this practice for yourself. For this specific session, commune with your inner Word Witch, Creative Spirit, or your intuition. See what you might discover about yourself as a writer by tapping into this subconscious place inside yourself.

To complete this ritual, consider the following five steps:

Step One: Set your intention for your practice. Return to our section on intentions if you need support in crafting your intent.

Step Two: Create an anchor statement and write it at the top of your page so you can easily refer to it. An anchor statement is a single line repeated over and over until the words begin to flow. It can work as a repetitive litany, an opening, or a phrase to return to if you lose your train of thought over the exercise.

If you need an anchor statement, I offer you one of these for your practice.

"My intuition speaks and says..."

"My inner Word Witch wants to share..."

"Dear Creative Spirit..."

Step Three: Set a timer and light a candle on your altar. I like to aim for around eleven minutes, but whatever feels like a manageable time for you will be perfect.

Step Four: Write continuously and without pause, allowing your words to flow without trying to "make sense" of them. These pages are just for you, so feel free to express yourself without judgment or fear. If you're able to write by hand, that's the preferred method. See how your handwriting shifts and changes throughout the exercises. If you don't know what to say, return to your anchor phrase, but do not pick your hand up from the piece of paper until you hear the timer go off.

Step Five: Reread and reflect on your writing. Occasionally, I like to sleep on it or revisit it at a later date to let the messages take on new meaning. After you're done writing, you might see a spark shine through your lines, a lantern, a fire of illumination and inspiration.

Bypassing your waking mind and quieting that voice of judgment that creeps in is essential to this practice. Judgment is a narrow view. This voice quiets the song of creativity. It dims the lantern that acts as the illuminating guide. This is an important notion to hold in your heart while you practice this ritual.

Write using this ritual and maybe you'll unlock the first line of your next poem or a way through the writer's block you've been facing. You can try this exercise again and again, shifting your intention and using it as a tool in your writing ritual toolbox to access that subconscious part of yourself. This practice is the flint and the tinder; it can build the most magical metaphorical fire in your Word Witch practice.

Journaling Prompts for Your Word Witch Journal

1. What symbols in nature remind you of the element of fire?
2. What can the pinecones and seeds that need fire teach you about your creative practice?
3. What is your first memory of believing in magic? What does the landscape of your childhood imagination look and feel like?
4. What do you desire in your creative practice?
5. What did it feel like to dance to a song you loved when you were thirteen? How do poetry, language, and magic live in the body?
6. What aspect of the story of Vasilisa and Baba Yaga were you most drawn to?
7. What do the doll and the skull of fire symbolize for you?
8. Read or listen to a recording of Lucille Clifton reading. Write about it.
9. What did you discover in your automatic writing practice?

Chapter Six

WATER

Calling Upon Cycles and the Phases of the Moon, the Seasons

The Water Element

Direction: the west
Symbolic Magic: a goblet, chalice, dish of water, moon water, seashell, river rock
Associations: emotions, depth, lineage, storytellers, stories, flow
The Ritual: cycles of creativity

Word Witches know the power of connecting with their creative cycles. Water is associated with the west, the direction of stories, emotions, intuition, and cyclicality. Water teaches us flow. Water is the guide that teaches the power of cyclicality in all things. I live by the light of the moon, guided by the seasons. These sacred cycles are the spiral that guides me forward, that inspires my work. In this chapter, you'll connect with the moon's cycles and the seasons to structure your creative process.

Approximately 70 percent of the earth's surface is covered in water, and about 60 percent of the average human body is composed of water. Because of this, according to psychosomatic therapist, herbalist, and author Heidi Smith, the body is like a tuning fork, allowing the water within us to connect with the water on our planet.[1] This water passes through our very bodies and becomes rainstorms, oceans, puddles underfoot. Everything is connected.

According to NASA, "Over billions of years, countless comets and asteroids have collided with Earth, enriching our planet with water. Chemical markers in the water of our oceans suggest that most of the water came from asteroids."[2] The fact that water arrived here and became a stable, life-giving source (unlike the other water that exists in our solar system to our knowledge) and, beyond that, the fact that our temperatures and atmosphere evolved to support water, not frozen, not boiling, but teeming with life is a deep well of inspiration.

Sit by any river, lake, or ocean, and take in the spirit of the place. See how the water rushes, watch a tide come in or out, and if you can, go swimming. I was lucky enough to visit La Fortuna waterfall in Costa Rica just as the space became open to visitors, first thing in the morning on a Pisces new moon during my honeymoon. As I held my breath and pushed off from the rocks toward the cascading water, I felt the magic of the place, the renewing energy. The power that water carries. Once, when I was young, on the North Sea in Old Hunstanton, England, I walked with my family along the beach by the bluffs as the tide went out. I said hello to the starfish, waiting patiently for the water to come back. The receding water changed the horizon, and the cycles of the water changed the landscape, evidenced by those bluffs and nearby cliffs.

Another favorite way to experience the magic of water is to sit on a porch or open a window during a rainstorm. Once, when I was staying in a renovated chicken coop in a holler in Knoxville for a writing residency with Sundress Publications, the remnants of a hurricane blew over the mountains. I sat in the hut with my dog, writing, as the walnuts from the tree nearby hit the tin roof throughout the night. I kept the fire burning and watched how the trees moved under the weight of the rain. I felt myself, a part of the cycle, and the water fueled my writing, my poems. You might get a little wet as the wind changes, but the experience of feeling the rain cycle in action is nothing short of a miracle. As you listen and watch, what might the water share with you? What memories of water rise to meet you now like the tides?

Water is our oceans, our tides, life giving,
life taking away, a force to be reckoned with,
ancient, pooling, cyclical.

One of the first cycles I remember learning about was the rain cycle: watching our puddles on the driveway evaporate into the clouds above, then fall back to the earth in a summer thunderstorm. The next cycle I learned about was the moon's journey, waxing to waning, full to new. The moon and the water on earth are ancient partners. They dance together around our planet as guides and teachers. The moon controls the tides; the water of the tides are woven into the rain cycle.

Water is an active guide in our writing. Intuitive artist and teacher Xenia Viray says, "Water also retains memory. Water, in its way, is also a collaborative artist, a mirror for life at all levels."[3] We can work with water to create.

Some scientists believe life began in the ocean 3.5 billion years ago. Myths mirror this story. Look through the pages of books, turn to the beginning, and you'll find water. Water is an origin place for stories. It is the place of our collective memory.

✸ *Word Witches know that writing is tidal, a cycle.* ✸

Living a writing life is like a rain cycle. The words and the practice don't show up in the same form each time, but each stage of the process is essential: repetition, returning to the page, allowing creativity to ebb and flow like water, arriving at the shore at high tide, gentle at first and then more persistent.

·•☽ Water on Your Word Witch Altar ☾•·

Water can be added to an altar in many forms. You might feel called to add a dish of water, a goblet, or a chalice. You might leave water out under different moon phases to create moon water and then anoint your altar with this lunar magic, or you might feel called instead to adorn your space with seashells, blue stones, or a rock you found in a sacred river, one that is close to your heart.

Once you decide on your symbol for the water, place it in the west-facing place of your altar, and consider how it relates to what you've placed in the south for fire and the east for air. You're building the circle, the spiral on your altar, with each choice and each intention.

Ritual:
·•☽ Water Magic ☾•·

Once you have chosen your talisman symbolic of water, I'd invite you to take out your Word Witch journal and write about your choice. Why have you chosen this object? And what story does it have to share with you? If it's more supportive, consider some questions you might ask the sacred water and write them out. Water is a teacher of old stories, so you can scry over the depths and see what the water offers you. Water teaches us to live, write, and make—all in flow.

To get started, consider reflecting on one or more of these prompts:

1. How did you choose your representation of water for your altar?
2. How do you see water connected to the fire and the air on your altar?
3. When you put the water on your altar, how do you feel? Why did you select this object to support you on your creative journey?

Ritual: Calling Upon Cycles in Your Writing Practice

In a Word Witch writing practice, when we speak about water, we must always speak about the moon. Just as the moon guides the tides, the lunar cycle can teach us many things about how to work cyclically and, in doing so, be a wonderful guide for our creativity. The moon compels the water of our practice, to move in cyclical ways.

The moon is celestial magic, rhythmic magic, tidal magic, both steady and untamed. The moon is a ritual anchor. The moon is a guide. Find the moon's presence in the sky, and you'll feel its soft glow, its supportive glow, its connection to all that is mystical.

In *The Moon Book: Lunar Magic to Change Your Life*, Sarah Faith Gottesdiener writes, "In astrology, psychology, and some magical traditions, the moon represents the subconscious. The subconscious is a source of our yearning and fear; it is where the stories and motivations behind our conscious behavior reveal themselves. When we decide to program our subconscious we change our beliefs. When we change our beliefs, our behavior changes. When our behavior changes, our life changes."[4]

Working with the moon is a way to shift your life and your practices to access a place of creativity and stories and dreams. Moon work is writing work and is the work of the Word Witch.

There are many differing opinions about the partnership between magic and the moon, but always remember that the most potent connections will be the ones you make for yourself. Use the open spaces in your Word Witch journal to reflect on how you feel while the moon is in different phases, transiting through different signs. Track your mood, creativity, and energy by writing a single sentence each day while you travel through this cycle, and pay attention to any patterns that arise. The moon is a powerful guide and teacher on your journey in creativity, and connection to her many phases are always a potent place to turn to in your writing rituals.

✸ *The moon is a sacred collaborator of the Word Witch.* ✸

·•☽ The Cycles of the Moon ☾•·

New Moon

The new moon is the first day of the new lunar cycle. This happens when the moon meets with the sun in the sky. This phase is linked with the dark moon. The dark moon is the final three days of the lunar cycle, as the moon appears to go dark, before it is renewed with the seed of the new moon. As beginnings and endings are always intertwined; this is part of the magic of the circle. The new moon is all about the new dream. This is a time of working with a beginning, taking the first step. During the new moon, consider your intentions and the seeds you'd like to tend to (metaphorically), dream, scheme, plot, and plan that you will nurture over the course of a moon cycle (or many moon cycles).

In a writing practice, this is an excellent time for conceptualizing a new project, for thinking about the beginnings of things. This is also an ideal time to make an outline, to free write about the potential or possibility of a project, or to ask the moon to offer you a bit of inspiration in the form of an idea you can write about.

Waxing Crescent

As the moon grows, so can your plans and intentions. The waxing crescent moon is a phase approximately between days two and six of the cycle. Connecting with the waxing crescent phase in your rituals helps you build momentum as you begin a new process or project.

In a writing practice, this is a potent time to ramp up your writing commitments and to hone your focus as you lovingly craft from your foundation. This is when you can begin to really put the work in, working toward all that is expanding in your writing, unfurling like the moon into the sky.

First Quarter

A first quarter moon phase is approximately between days six and nine of the lunar cycle. Much like the waxing crescent, this phase can help you work toward your goals, develop strong habits, and move through processes. How do you show up daily or weekly to your writing projects? Consider setting goals or intentions within your larger framework to help you work toward the ultimate goal in a more manageable way.

In a writing practice, this is a potent time to consider what's working and to continue following that thread. This is also a good time in the lunar cycle to consider how your habits ripple out beyond even what you're currently working on, and reflect upon who you are in your hard work and dedication to your craft.

Waxing Gibbous

The waxing gibbous moon phase is approximately between days nine and thirteen of the lunar cycle. When you connect with the waxing gibbous phase, you can enhance your spells and rituals with growth, abundance, and expansion.

In a writing practice, this is a moment to celebrate the work you've created so far in your project. It allows you to be present with all that already is and open yourself to the possibility of what comes next. Give thanks to the creativity that has already manifested in your practice as you move toward the ever-potent full moon in the sky.

Full Moon

The full moon phase is approximately between days thirteen and fifteen of the cycle, when the moon is exactly opposite the sun in the sky. The full moon celebrates wholeness, fulfillment, sensuality, and abundance magic.

In a writing practice, the full moon marks a culmination. This can be an ideal moment to finish a project, celebrate a project, release anything holding you back from your writing practice, illuminate something in your work, or honor the wholeness of who you are as a writer.

Waning Gibbous

The waning gibbous moon is approximately between days fifteen and twenty-one of the cycle. When you connect your magic with the waning gibbous phase, you can integrate the lessons of the full moon, deepen your understanding, and continue to release that which is no longer serving you.

In a writing practice, the waning gibbous empowers you to continue shedding any old stories that would hold you back as the cycle repeats itself. It also allows you to integrate and better understand your internal cycles, for example, when you feel most generative and creative, or when you feel like you're better able to work through big picture ideas. This can also give us insights into when we might need to plan to rest in our practice.

Last Quarter

The last quarter phase is approximately between days twenty-one and twenty-three of the moon cycle. By connecting with a last quarter moon, you can turn inward and reflect. This is a great moon for working through the subconscious and shadow work.

If anything in the subconscious is holding you back, this is a great moment to work through that, call upon shadow work around your creativity, or review and take stock of all you've created thus far.

Waning Crescent

The waning crescent phase is approximately between days twenty-three and twenty-seven of the cycle. The waning crescent phase can help you clean, clear, purify, banish, and release. Under the darkening moon, you can connect more and more with that which is liminal and intuitive for you.

In a writing practice, the waning crescent moon allows you to deepen your intuition as a writer. If there are any places in your work where you've felt stuck or blocked in the past, now is the moment to work with your intuition (maybe through automatic writing) to write through it. Sometimes your intuition knows where a project should travel before your conscious mind does.

Dark Moon

The dark moon marks the end of the lunar cycle before it begins again, connected with the new moon, and it takes place at approximately days twenty-seven to twenty-nine of the cycle. The dark moon asks you to turn inward, to reflect and rest. The dark moon is the time of the Goddess, when the moon appears to go dark in the sky, mirroring a moment of hermit-like magic, where we can be reclusive in our work.

The dark moon is plutonian, chthonic, and confronting. This phase asks you to rest in the cocoon of the dark before the moon begins again. Remember that rest is an essential part of the writing process. As you rest, you might dream, and as you dream, you might find the next seed to be planted on the new moon.[5]

The Seasonal Cycles

Much like the moon cycles, the year turns through the seasons. In neo-paganism, this is called the Wheel of the Year. The earth-based holidays, or "spokes" on this wheel, are the solstices, equinoxes, and the cross-quarter days. The cross-quarter days are the four holidays that are suspended in the balance between these earth-based holidays. Broader than the moon cycles, the cycles of the seasons can teach us about the energy of the year at large. The seasons can help us live our lives cyclically, and to work in collaboration with the earth. Even if we live in a place where seasons are not as starkly delineated, marking this time energetically can be incredibly supportive in your practice as a Word Witch.

Much like honoring moon cycles, the most important associations are the ones that we make for ourselves. Spring may look different in the desert than it does in the jungle. You may feel different creatively in summer than someone else you collaborate with. Your seasons are your seasons; celebrate how they ebb and flow.

Word Witches dance with the
sacred spiral of the seasons.

The Spring Equinox

To me, the spring equinox marks the beginning of the year. While some consider winter solstice or even Samhain to be the Witch's New Year, I believe the beginning happens with the first sign of the zodiac, Aries, as it ushers in the astrological new year. The spring equinox is all about planting seeds, about the softening of the earth, about the grief that rises to the top of the soil after all is revealed from winter and laid bare. It is also about where death and rebirth meet on the cycle.

In a writing practice, this is similar to the new moon time. It is a moment to conceptualize your ideas, to grieve or release old stories, to clean out the garden beds, and to be ready for the spring rains and the softening of soil in your writing. If you keep a garden yourself, you might whisper your writing ideas or projects to your seedlings and ask them to help you as you create over the course of the year. If you live in an apartment like I do, consider this ritual with a houseplant instead. The seed can also be imaginary; it can live on the page, it can live in your heart, or in your head.

Aries is also a cardinal fire sign, meaning it is ruled by the element of fire and appears at the beginning of a season. This cardinal fire energy is galvanizing, supportive, and great at getting the ball rolling, so to speak. So it can be a great ally and energy for a fresh start.

Beltane

Beltane appears on the calendar in the northern hemisphere on or around May 1. It takes place in the balance between equinox and solstice. In some places, it might be when the hawthorn blossoms appear again. In others, it's when you feel the fairies return to your garden. Beltane is a moment of rising energy. It is the blooming flowers, the ground now fully thawed and accepting of the rains. *To me, Beltane is sensuality, unfurling. It is heading for the woods to go seek your wild.*

In a writing practice, I see this time resonating with the waxing crescent, giving you the boost you need to move through your work energetically. This is a gathering moment. You might find your metaphorical basket filled with the new blooms of ideas. You will want to tend to the symbolic garden as it gathers steam. This is a time to make lists and create outlines to support your ideas that were just seeds at the new moon. This is also a time to reflect on your inherent creativity as a bit of magic tied to the rest of the world.

The Summer Solstice

The summer solstice happens when the sun moves into Cancer and summer is at its peak here in the northern hemisphere in the days around June 20. This is a culminating moment, the longest day of the year. The sun dances into the later night. The mugwort is in full abundance. The energy is high; hopefully you're spending time celebrating the sun with your family and community. This is a moment of festivity. Summer solstice asks you to celebrate your achievements so far.

In a creative practice, this is a first quarter moon. The energy will continue to build in your projects. Maybe you have noticed that you're gaining momentum, and magic seems abundant in all you write. As your intuition sharpens, you might generate work that you can then edit later. Working *with* this building energy can allow you to feel supported as you write. Perhaps you'll even want to take your writing out under the moon on the solstice and ask the moon to bless your words with summer magic.

Lughnasadh

Lughnasadh is the beginning of the harvest season. Happening on or around August 1, this is a cross-quarter day in the balance of solstice and equinox. The work that began as a mere seed is just beginning to come to fruition, and now is the time to really get to work. If there is pruning or weeding or harvesting to be done, start the process. Lughnasadh is also sometimes called first harvest. In this moment, summer has reached its final forms, fall feels just on the horizon, and the land is changing.

In a writing practice, this is like the waxing gibbous moon phase. You might feel like you're beginning to reach a sort of wholeness. As you look ahead toward the completion of a project, this is a moment of reflection. Look back and celebrate all the moments of hard work that have brought you to where you are. *And keep writing!* You're almost finished with your project. Edit where necessary.

The Autumn Equinox

The autumn equinox, sometimes called Mabon, is when the sun moves into Libra season on or around September 20. This is the second harvest. The world is in its abundance. Hopefully the work you've put in during the year, beginning at the spring equinox, has allowed you to stock your pantries full (metaphorical or otherwise). During the second harvest, you might feel called to gather, or celebrate, the warmth of summer in the northern hemisphere as it still lingers in these early fall days. Put your face to the sun to fully absorb the rays of light that shine down upon you, throw a gratitude gathering with friends, and enjoy the last moments of warmth, before fall fully embraces the land.

In a writing practice, this is a full moon moment. What is culminating? Are your hands full with the abundance of your words? *Look at all the work you've put in!* You've completed your writing project and your cup overflows.

Samhain

Samhain is also sometimes called the Witch's New Year and takes place around the holiday that many refer to as Halloween.

Sometimes it's on the day after Halloween, aligned with Dia de los Muertos, or All Souls' Day; other times it's astrologically aligned with the sun at fifteen degrees of Scorpio, between equinox and solstice. No matter when you celebrate this sacred day, it's a time to honor the dead. During Samhain, the days darken and we stand at the gate of winter. This is a seasonal shift, a reminder that we must find our resilience to persevere through the dark days ahead. During this time, the otherworld draws close; make altars adorned with marigolds to honor the ancestors, feel yourself standing on the threshold of the shadow months, winter is arriving at the door.

In your writing practice, this is a waning gibbous moment. As the energy shifts from the full abundance of the autumn equinox, the air begins to carry a chill. Samhain asks you to deepen and listen to your intuition. If you have questions about what a project might become, how to edit the project, or where the project must travel for it to reach completion, *this* is the energy you want to work with. Many say the "veil is thin" during this time; however, the origins of this saying are not as ancient as some might think (it's a discussion among witchy circles!). That doesn't mean that it isn't true. The spirit world draws close at threshold moments, and Samhain is one of them. *Tend to your Word Witch altar and seek answers in your dreams.*

The Winter Solstice

The winter solstice happens in the northern hemisphere as the sun shifts into the sign of Capricorn on or around December 20. This is the darkest and longest night of the year. Under the cloak of this darkness, you can turn inward and reflect. To me, the winter solstice represents the candle placed in the window, while the spirits of our beloved ancestors pass by. Some consider this to mark a new year, a creative cocoon, a moment that prompts you to reflect on your resiliency. The winter solstice asks you to remember that light comes from within, even as the shadows and cold may waltz through the air.

In your writing practice, this is similar to a last quarter moon. Your editing must become serious as you read through new lenses and by candlelight. You must confront the shadows in your work, asking them if they are hungry or lonely, or if they are just passing through. You can clear the way toward completion under this last quarter moon, refining the piece that you set out to make the previous spring. *The editorial eye is a different kind of art.*

Imbolc

Imbolc is the cross-quarter day between winter solstice and the spring equinox. With many pieces of lore surrounding this sacred moment on or around February 1, some associate it with the Irish goddess turned patron saint Brigid. Brigid is a goddess of blacksmithing, poetry, healing waters, and fire divine. She is a protector of the young and of the more-than-human world. Others say that this day happens when the wolves mate or the sheep need to be tended to. Imbolc is also associated with the American tradition of Groundhog's Day, when you anticipate the arrival of spring.

In your writing practice, this is like a waning crescent into the dark moon times before spring. The waning crescent slips into the darkness of the three days that precede a new moon, much like Imbolc does before spring. Cycles don't end and begin at exact points, but rather as a gradient. The wheel is always turning; the seasons are always changing.

Imbolc is the time to embrace the ending of a project or an approach to a project you've been taking. Of course, some projects extend beyond an annual cycle. But before spring comes again, close a chapter. The dark moon is a sacred time where only the dream of the dream exists. Find ways in your writing practice to embrace these ideas coexisting together. Like the symbolic ouroboros, the snake eating its tail, the days spiral into each other as you write and write again.

•●○●•

These moon and seasonal cycles repeat many times in a writing life or a writing practice. Everyone is different in their cycles and seasons, but by paying attention, you will learn so much from them, and you'll be able to figure out how to use them to enhance your practice as a Word Witch.

Journaling Prompts for Your Word Witch Journal

1. What symbols in nature remind you of the element of water?
2. Spend some time with water (a lake, a river, a rainstorm) and sit quietly and listen. What does the water share with you?
3. What does the symbol of the moon mean to you? What associations do you feel with the tides or rain cycle?
4. When do you feel the most in flow and connected to your cycles in the writing process?
5. Spend the next month writing one sentence about the phase the moon is in and how you feel creatively. What do you notice?
6. Write how you feel in each season from a creative perspective. Does your map match with mine, or does it guide you to do something different?
7. What do you notice in nature to signal the arrival of each season? What do these harbingers teach you?

Chapter Seven

EARTH

Inspiration, Reciprocity, Observation,
Poetry, and Song

The Earth Element

Direction: the north
Symbolic Magic: dirt, herbs, tree branches, rocks, crystals, leaves
Associations: connection, guardians, roots
Ritual: paying attention, song, poetry

The Word Witch is connected to the earth, is of the earth, and knows that the heart of a writing practice comes from being a part of this wild and beautiful planet. One of the most essential tenets and guides to being a Witch is to be a guardian and steward of this planet. Protect our home, and our home will protect us. Love the earth, and the earth will love us in return.

Earth is the echo of every poem we sing into the metaphorical mountains. Earth is the gentle guide of our practices, home to our air, fire, and water. *How lucky are we to exist at all?* What a blessing to be of this earth.

Nature is a metaphor for many creative acts, but even that, the earth is creativity. Look at giraffes or the spiral of a fern, listen to a robin's song, or watch a sunflower bloom. This is creativity in every sense of the word. The writing practice of the Word Witch is inherently grounded in the earth. In magic and ritual, earth is associated with the north, the direction of connection, more than human beings, plant kin, guardian trees, sacred dirt and stones, and being rooted.

In this chapter, we'll first discuss the physical gifts of the earth that can be used to create an altar and then pair it with a ritual. The earth on your altar can symbolize all that is grounded in your practice and all that is connected—green, fertile, and cyclical. Next we'll explore how we can partner the gifts that the earth offers us, such as the rhythms of the seasons, with ritual. Then we'll discuss poetry and songs, gifts that the earth gives us for our Word Witch practice, and we'll discover how weaving in poetic sensibilities, singing aloud, and lyrics can deepen our connection with the element of earth.

Earth on Your Word Witch Altar

The earth is filled with natural gifts. You are a gift, as you are of this earth. Beyond that, observe your surroundings and you'll notice that these presents are everywhere, in ever-growing abundance.

If you've ever walked through a forest and picked up an acorn to keep in your pocket, strolled along the edge of the ocean and found a shell that now rests on the dashboard of your car, or picked up a smooth stone from a river and rubbed it between your fingers, then you've received a gift from the earth.

A gift of the earth can be the gift of nourishment. I remember my dad growing tomatoes in the garden and eating them, warm with sun, and adding only salt. The basil my mom would harvest from the garden ended up on top of spaghetti, or the mint she grew chopped into salads. The gift can also be beauty. There used to be a lilac tree at my mom's house, and I remember the purple flowers as they sat in a vase, or the peonies that lined the garage that my sister and I would commune with, as the ants made their yearly pilgrimage to these blossoms (ants and peonies have a beautiful symbiotic relationship). My neighbors that grow roses here in Brooklyn are a special kind of magic maker. I am sure to thank these roses as I pass by on my way to the corner store or the park; they are amulets of earth magic in the middle of the bustling city.

When I was young, I started one of my favorite and first collections of earth-given gifts with my mom. From the pages of one of the fairy books we read together, we discovered fairy stones: rocks with a ring around them are considered good luck. We scoured the ground looking for them, and as we picked them up, we whispered our various acknowledgments and blessings to the earth spirits who created them. Ever since then, when the conditions are just right, and I can feel the smooth stone of a river, creek, or landscape wants to come home in my pocket, I take them with me. Stones hold a certain kind of magic, and there are many traditions of magical rocks. Fairy stones, like hagstones (a stone with a hole worn through), are another gift from the earth and are thought to give the beholder the ability to peer between worlds.

Not all gifts from the earth are things you can take and place on an altar. Some sites are sacred and not meant to be touched; sometimes the earth wishes her stones to remain where you found them. A Word Witch creates rituals with care for the planet, always with the deep understanding that everything is connected, and we must be gentle stewards. That's why "asking permission" from the earth and respecting the concept of reciprocity are essential practices for any Word Witch.

Word Witches are stewards
and guardians of our planet.

Asking Permission and Reciprocity

I always ask the earth before harvesting any herb or taking anything from the natural world. Green Witch Robin Rose Bennett's work is indispensable in this area and was formative in my understanding of reciprocity.[1] These teachings are also foundational in Indigenous and earth-based religions and spiritualities and have been discussed by many others, such as intuitive plant herbalist Asia Suler,[2] author Robin Wall Kimmerer, and Indigenous herbalist and author Felicia Cocotzin Ruiz.[3] While the language varies, and every practice is unique to the individual practitioner and their lineage, a common thread of importance is the knowledge that we are all part of a delicate balance and that consumption culture, of taking without regard to this fragile organism, would be a disservice to our magic and our connection to the planet.

I always look for this guiding language in my study of the earth. It's essential to begin our rituals of earth with listening and love. During my Green Witch apprenticeship, Robin would have us listen to the plants before harvesting, asking them, "Do I have permission?" We would ask and thank the plant for sharing its medicine in the part we are harvesting and to bring its energy back into itself. It is always best magical practice to leave a gift in return, what Robin lovingly calls "giveaways." There are many ways to reciprocate the earth's generosity and practice a small ritual of thanks. I keep a tin on my person for this reason. Anytime I take something from my natural surroundings, I leave a piece of cedar in return as a quiet acknowledgment of gratitude. I chose cedar because cedar is a tree with which I have always had a special relationship, ever since my childhood in Michigan. I also found it to be one of my allies during my apprenticeship, which makes sense since it's also known for its grandmotherly and protective energy. I suggest choosing a similar gift of thanks that feels true to you and your roots. It can be a single herb, as I have chosen, or it can be a blend of plants, crafted with loving intention, to guide you in a reciprocal relationship with the earth. In a pinch, or if leaving anything behind isn't a wise choice, a song, a poem, or a blessing of thanks can also work beautifully.

To ask permission to take a stone, a leaf, or any of earth's gifts is quite simple. Focus your energy and ask the earth if taking the item with you is okay. If the plant, tree, spirit, earth, says yes, you're welcome to harvest, but in the words of Robin Wall Kimmerer, as she reminds us in her "Honorable Harvest" guidelines in the book *Braiding Sweetgrass*: "Never take the first, never take the last, and take only what you need."[4]

Sometimes when you ask for permission, your request might be denied—and you might wonder why. Sometimes a seashell must return to the ocean. Sometimes the acorn must be planted. Have faith that there is a reason behind it, even if you don't know what the reason is yet.

These practices of reciprocity, right relationship, earth stewardship, and understanding and care for all aspects of our planet are directly related to our work as creative beings. The craft of the Word Witch is one of being connected and paying attention. Without an intention of love for our home, without a desire to cultivate care and enchantment on earth, there would be no witchcraft or magic, and there would be no creativity. This is the wellspring of inspiration, our guiding north start in our practice as Witch and writer.

The Word Witch knows the earth is the embodiment of creativity.

Ritual:
Offering Attention

One of the foundational practices of both witchcraft *and* writing is offering or gifting your attention to the world around you. Seeking stillness whenever we can helps us better understand our world. And when I say stillness, I don't necessarily mean the stillness of staying put, but rather the potential of solitude and the quietude that it takes to listen. A certain stillness and sharpness of the mind is needed to truly see the world.

Amid the chaos of our daily lives, it doesn't always seem practical. However, in what Mary Oliver calls "the five rivers," her delectable poem about plum trees, "The Plum Trees," she reminds us that it's *always* possible to call on the senses (whichever we have at our disposal) to experience our surroundings better.[5] To inundate your senses and allow yourself to experience all the joyous and sensuous gifts of this earth is fodder for your creative practice. Delight in being alive. I have always found that when I am experiencing more joy and ease, I can write better and more clearly, with love and understanding for my life.

When walking down the sidewalk, raise your head toward the sky. You may see a crow, hear a trickle of water, or notice the rush of a busy intersection in the distance. Perhaps you smell freshly baked bread or the fields of hay, depending on where you live, or maybe you feel the metal of a railing, the soft fur of a dog you've stopped to pet as you greet your neighbor, or the slightest touch of a single hair against your cheek. These seemingly small moments, strung together, make up a life—and even the most minute detail can inform our witchcraft and writing practices. When my grandpa died, my aunt and I started seeing mourning doves everywhere, and now when I see them, I think of that time in my life. My grandma's friend Karla, the bookshop keeper and intuitive, once told me wisely, "If a Witch sees something once they pay attention, if they see something twice they know it's important, but if a Witch sees something three times, then they know someone is trying to get their attention." There is profound magic when you notice something and begin to see it everywhere.

When I am traveling, I try to write a poem every day. These poems are not so much about the craft but, instead, the impulse of documenting, experiencing through language the power and potency of recording an experience. After my travels are long over and I've returned home, I can still feel the cold air of Alaska, hear the dolphins during a storm in the Florida Keys, or eat a grilled cheese at a diner somewhere in North Dakota as we drive across the country. These scraps of Word Witchery commemorate the rich experience of being alive and on earth.

Nature is an oracle. And we are, too, naturally. We are radically present when we slow down and pay attention to the world around us. We aren't looking at our cell phones, lost in a mess of digital wires or crisscrossing text messages. We aren't worried about getting here or there, catching the train, or hitting a red light. We are of the world. The creative process can be taught to you in the way that the light refracts off the East River in New York, the way the city looks as the J train crosses over the Williamsburg Bridge, the way a deer bows when it's nervous, or the way a red-tailed hawk moves through the sky.

Witches know that radical presence is a form of ritual in and of itself—and through creativity, we can outwardly express all that we've observed. Being present is a radical act in a world that wants to steal your attention for the economy. Reclaim your attention and put it into your magic and your poetry.

Consider keeping a note in your phone or a journal in your bag where you can record your daily witnessing. It can be as simple a list as this: pigeon eating a french fry, dog that smiles, beautiful pink sky, the Empire State Building across the water, the way my love holds a spatula while cooking, the smell of a candle on a January night. Through keeping this list, you will have a running log of everything you've seen that you have given your attention to. You will be able to fill a cauldron with ingredients to make the most healing metaphorical soup, and you will have a well from which to draw every time you write.

I think about the poet and farmer Ross Gay, who had a daily practice of writing essays in which he found delight in his daily life, which he then published as *The Book of Delights*. These essays demonstrated that the more he looked for delight, the more he found. He said, "It didn't take me long to learn that the discipline or practice of writing these essays occasioned a kind of delight radar. Or maybe it was more like the development of a delight muscle. Something that implies that the more you study delight, the more delight there is to study."[6] Word Witches know that delight and joy come from the creative energy of the earth.

Word Witches yearn to be enchanted. To do so, simply acknowledge the world around us, and follow the wise words of Mary Oliver: "Instructions for living a life. / Pay attention. / Be astonished. / Tell about it."[7]

Whenever you feel disconnected from your creativity, magic, or craft, you can reread your running list and feel astonished at all you have seen. Then you must "tell about it," and take out your pen to write. It doesn't need to be anything fancy: Write a simple sentence talking about exactly what you saw, and then see how that is a poem.

·•☽ Earth on Your Word Witch Altar ☾•·

To select an earth element symbol to bring to your Word Witch altar, I invite you to go on a ritual walk in a place that is significant to you. This can be somewhere you visit frequently, like a nearby park or backyard, or you can go on an intentional hike to a spot in your community where you feel grounded and connected to the earth. Before you go on this walk, set an intention to find an item that can bring the element of earth to your altar, keep your creative practice grounded, and remind you where you write from and who you write for.

You can either state this intention aloud or write it on a slip of paper to put in your pocket while you walk. Whenever you find your stone, bone, leaf, acorn, shell, or other gift of the earth, practice asking permission and leaving a small gift in return and reciprocity. When you're ready, place this on the north-facing aspect of your altar. Feel how it's in conversation with the water you've placed in the west, the fire symbol you've added to the south, and the air you've added to the east. How do you feel about the energy of your circle and the sacred spiral?

Ritual:
·•☽ Earth Magic ☾•·

Once you have chosen your earthly talisman for your Word Witch practice, I invite you to take out your Word Witch journal and write about your choice. Why have you chosen this object? And what story does it have to share with you? Consider some questions you might ask this gift from the earth about your role as a writer and a Word Witch on this planet. Earth keeps us grounded, reminding us that we're all connected through the web of life. It also teaches us lessons about more-than-human kin, presence, and dedication.

To get started, consider reflecting on one or more of these prompts:

1. What did you discover on your ritual walk? And what gift did you bring home to put on your altar?
2. How did you know this object was meant to be on your Word Witch altar?
3. How does earth symbolically appear in your journey as a writer? How do you see it related to the water, fire, and air?
4. What would it feel like to be grounded in your writing and other creative work?

Metaphorical Gifts from the Earth for Your Creative Practice

There are many ways to connect to the earth, but one of the most valuable in my practice is offering my attention to the world around me. When I first moved to Brooklyn, I was surprised to find datura, or moonflower, lining the city sidewalks. The more I paid attention to these intoxicating white, night-blooming flowers, the more I noticed. As I would walk the sidewalks with my friends, I would gesture to them and say, *"Meet Datura,"* a flower that has inspired many myths and may have been involved in the rituals of the Delphic Oracles. Stories are everywhere, just waiting for us to pay attention.

This ritual of attention has been a source of inspiration not just in Brooklyn but throughout my relationships and life. Last week, when visiting Michigan, my cousin Hannah told me about spotting a dogwood tree outside of a church, describing it as a tree of white stars. *This was a delight to hear.* Today, even after living in orbit with my mom's house, my childhood home since I was five, I saw the familiar elder tree bloom in a new way. This attention is a gift, not just to the earth but to us.

It's not always a subtle gift, either. A teacher once told me that she had a neighbor who would run out into his yard every morning and strike a gong, yelling, "Pay attention. Pay attention. Your life is moving very quickly." And perhaps we all need that resonant reminder as we move through our lives, to slow down and look outside of ourselves.

Growing up, I used to go on adventures with my Aunt Kathryn and Uncle Norman. Though not related by blood, they were born to me by something deeper: *love.* Whenever we would pull away from my house, they would gesture to the neighbor's lawn, and my Aunt Kathryn (a retired English teacher) would say to whoever was in the car, "Class, look at the myrtle." She was teaching us that the world was a classroom and that even the crawling green on the neighbor's lawn contained magic if only we cared to notice.

Often, in a hurried world, it is easy to rush by these gifts and unknowingly miss the deer scapula left on the side of a hiking trail, the hawk's nest above the track in the park, and the light refracting through a window to make a shadow on your wall. However, as a Word Witch, paying attention keeps you tethered to our shared experiences and allows you to experience presence.

There are many ways to cultivate a relationship with this earth-based energy. A simple strategy is to sit on the earth, lean against a tree, or go barefoot when the world's weight becomes overbearing. You can imagine a long cord running from the top of your head and into the earth, rooting you down, keeping you connected. Through that cord, any anxiety, sadness, or grief that you may have can travel down into the earth to be alchemized into something else. One of the teachers I've had even suggested asking for these feelings to be transformed into flowers. I also suggest poems.

When we pay attention to the earth, the earth speaks back. I first encountered Nobel laureate and Pulitzer Prize–winning poet Louise Glück while I was completing a fellowship at Pierce Cedar Creek Institute. In her poetry collection *The Wild Iris,* she explores life and death and what it means to be human, voiced by the beings that inhabit that world, such as "The Wild Iris," "Snow Drops," and "Red Poppy." In the title poem, the speaker, the iris, says that everything will again find a voice. The iris offers its voice as a storyteller for the poem, allowing the poet to tell a different story, to weave the earth's energy into the poem's words.[8]

For the summer in 2012 I participated in this fellowship, I lived and wrote alongside scientific researchers and created a manuscript titled *Voicing the Natural.* Guided by my mentor and poet Diane Seuss, I wandered about the woods and crafted a project, inspired by Glück's work, and also *The Fingernail of Luck* by Conrad Hilberry.[9] I followed the researchers as they examined the thermoregulation of dragonflies. I spent a day in a swamp with tongs, a pillowcase, and a paint bucket, capturing the massasauga rattlesnake for tagging. I stumbled across a decapitated deer in the woods; it was the most poignant metaphor I could find for what I was going through in my life emotionally at the time, and I grieved alongside this loss. In working on this project, I learned something important about the speakers of our creative work. Sometimes the speaker is us, sometimes it isn't, and sometimes it's something we channel, a story that originates from a different life.

The stories of the beings that we inhabit the earth with long to be told. I remember paddling a boat with two fellow researchers on Brewster Lake and watching the beaver at the other end of the water building a dam. The lake, the beaver, the trees, the stories of my fellow seekers, all contributed to the poems that wanted to be told. All I needed to do was listen. Taking my journal, each day, I foraged for the stories of the beings. I learned about the cleavers, burning prairie landscapes. Each path in the forest, each life, each death I encountered were not just fodder for writing but were the poems embodied. Nature, in her generosity, gifted me poems like one might pick an apple off a tree in fall. If you are ever feeling stuck or disconnected from your magic or your words, go to your window, sit outside, go for a walk. There is very little that I haven't been able to solve or at least make better momentarily by going for a walk. On this walk, you might even encounter visitors.

For example, if I were to step outside my apartment in New York City right now, I might see a rat scurry by, the cherry blossoms might be blooming, or a squirrel might dash through the dusk. All of these beings are collaborators and oracles on your Word Witch path. They might offer their voices to your writing. Close your eyes and allow them to speak through your words. What can the rat teach you about resilience? Does the squirrel have a lesson about the dusk itself, or what do the cherry blossoms sing about new beginnings? Voicing the natural is a project that any of us can seek, and in doing so, the earth sings through our work, a constant ritual and reminder of connectedness.

The earth is an incredible guide who knows how to help transform things into different versions of themselves. The more-than-human world is also a teacher of this. Butterflies, for example, know this innately.

When tucked inside their cocoons, caterpillars must first become a liquid version of themselves, allowing themselves to return to the very beginning—all before transformation can occur and they are reborn as butterflies.

What a beautiful lived experience of the creative process.

Sometimes, giving a piece of creative work to the earth can be the entire purpose of its creation. While teaching a master class at Sarah Lawrence College, poet and writer Bhanu Kapil explained how she once threw her manuscript into the winter landscape, where it sat in the snow for many months. When spring came, she returned to the bones of her text and unearthed messages that would become her book.[10]

I admire how fearlessly she turned her work over to the earth in this story. It stuck with me that she allowed the forces of winter and the elements to make this manuscript, her book, different from what she had created and found not quite right. I have given the ashes of many a poem or piece of writing to the earth in my backyard in Brooklyn, burying, releasing, dreaming in coordination with the soil.

The seasons themselves are a gift from the earth, reminding us that everything must come in cycles and that the process's beginning and end are often inextricably linked. Every season has its potency, teaches its lessons, and allows different earthly gifts, keeping us fed and supported, constantly nourished. We connected with these cycles during our lessons of water, but as we have seen, all the elements are connected, spiraling into each other. As we spiral through our circle, it is natural to turn backward within the spiral, before pivoting again forward. After working with the earth element, it might be a potent time to revisit the water chapter and see what you have discovered about your cycles since then.

Earth magic, in part, is connected to the roots that in turn connect us to each other and to the rest of the planet. When you're not sure where to go in your writing, turn to your roots. The roots are messy. The roots are dirt under the fingernails. They don't always come from trees; sometimes they are the small and multiple roots of oat straw, they are a taproot, they are a place, a person, a box under the bed. They are storied histories. The way we connect is also reaching, strange, gnarled. The roots are symbols for our own origin stories, our creation myths, our family lore. And these roots are just waiting to be honored in our Word Witch rituals.

Poetry

Poetry is a powerful practice of the Word Witch. Much like spells, poems are conjured, channeled, pieces of magic and stories. Poems are an impulse of being human. Poems are from the earth. The word poetry comes from the Greek word *poieo,* meaning "I create." *The poet is the maker.* The poet is the creator. The poet is a Word Witch. In much of my research about the origins of poetry, one thing was clear: Poetry predates literacy. I like to think of these original poems as great exclamations, as yips of joy or wails of grief. I like to think that this impulse to create comes from the core of being alive on this earth. The spirit of poems is directly linked to the soul. Knowing the history of these poems, I invite you in your Word Witch practice to create poetry in a way that feels authentic to yourself. Much of poetry is dedicated to the study of its craft, but your practice could instead start from tending to its creator, the poet inside of us. Wail loudly, sing, chant the poems from your stomach, your womb space, your root.

Of course, this isn't to say that studying poetry isn't important—technique, meter, careful editing, and questioning of the poem. But for those beginning on their path of Word Witchery, it's better to celebrate the creation of each poem you are called to bring into the world. It's more productive, allowing for more magic to connect to the practice of the creative act itself. This is one of the main reasons children are so inherently creative; they do not worry about making something good because it's an expression of how they interact with the world around them.

Ultimately, poetry allows us to connect to our humanity. The history of the poem is intertwined with the history of becoming human. The earliest poems were passed down through oral traditions. They were spoken, sung, or chanted, perhaps in sacred religious sites or sacred sites like around a fire before a meal. Poems make up the fabric of our histories. Read and write poems because you love language. Read and write poems because you love the world. As Pulitzer Prize–winning poet Marie Howe said, "I read poetry to stay alive. That's why I went to poetry in the first place, that's why I stay with it, that's why I'll never leave it."[11] I write poetry because it makes me remember. I write poetry because it gives me joy. I write poetry because it reminds me that I am both young and ancient. I write poems because I can't not write poems. I write poems because I am alive on earth. Poems come from the page, but beyond that, they come from the earth.

Beyond the vital act of writing your own poetry is the practice of reading another's poetry. Reading poetry can help you connect to the poet's landscape, introducing you to the different rhythms and orientation of the form. Reading poems brings together the offerings of all the other poets in the world who have written before you or who write alongside you. Whenever you read another's poetry, you realize you aren't alone on the path of the Word Witch, especially as you grapple with the same large and unwieldy ideas, in the same short amount of words. Concise and precise language are necessary tools.

More than anything else, it's about how the poem makes you feel—*that's* where the real magic is. As Emily Dickinson famously said, "If I read a book [and] it makes my whole body so cold no fire can ever warm me, I know that is poetry. If I feel physically as if the top of my head were taken off, I know that is poetry. These are the only ways I know it. Is there any other way."[12] I know I've read a poem when I feel a spark in my body. The spark is magic, whimsy, curiosity, a new question, a perspective, an old story, a myth, the corner of the mouth before it begins to smile. The spark is inspiration made real.

I invite you to go to the library, online, a friend's house, or even your own bookshelf and find a book of poems. Scan the pages until you feel a chill come over your body, the resonance between you and the words, which in your body you feel those mycelial-like connections. When you read a piece of prose like this, you can truly feel the magnitude of the poem brought to the altar of your life.

Whenever someone asks me why I study poetry and what I will "do with that," I smile and laugh—because I know a secret. Studying poetry is the most human thing we can do. Reading poetry reminds us of how we're all connected, how we all share human thoughts, and how we differ in perspectives. It uses the smallest number of words with careful precision to say "I was here."

So, Word Witch, how will you create poems that serve as an offering to those that read them? How will you allow yourself to be nourished by the offerings of other poets? It's always both. We must read *and* we must write, connected to others who are trying to make sense of the world just as we are.

In the essay "The Poet," written by Ralph Waldo Emerson, he tells us that "every word was once a poem."[13] I love to think about language like this. Each word carries a long tradition, being worked and reworked by the cultures that have used it, treasured it, strung it together like beads to make meaning, over the course of centuries and even millennia. Build relationships with each word as a poem. Build a relationship with the resonance between the words until you feel the poetry flow through your practice.

In many writing containers and communities, people will ask me, "Is this a poem?" And then, when I tell them, "If you think it's a poem, then it's a poem," the inevitable always follows: "Well, is the poem good?"

"Good" and "bad" are the lessons of disheartening classrooms and exist on an unhelpful binary; they exclude nuance, possibility, authenticity, creative impulse, and magic. This question ignores the fact that the poem itself is an offering to be left on the altar to communicate with the gods and all that is divine of earth.

Poems are doorways, pathways. Asking if they are "good" is like asking if a tree is "good," or if the soil is "good"; they are all different, generative, and alive. I am affirming through these pages right now that if you want to call a piece of writing a poem, and it felt empowering, creative, freeing, and human to create it, then yes, it was important that you wrote it—whether or not others might consider it to be "good" or "bad."

Write the poems. They will be your own, crafted from a lifetime of witchery, enchantment, and the wisdom the earth has imparted. Write them because they come to you, dreams, visions, visitors, waiting to be written.

✸ *The Word Witch is a poet.* ✸

Ritual: Writing a Poem

In one of the first online writing workshops I taught, I remember offering a prompt to encourage the writers to embark on their poetry writing journey. One of my dear friends was taking the class and messaged me on the side, saying, "This prompt is beautiful, but I'm not sure what I'm supposed to do with it. Where do I start to create the poem?"

And what a genius question this was. Even if we are in love with poems, feel the tops of our heads taken off, and are inspired to write, create, and converse with these ancient writers and prophecies, where do we begin? Louise Bourgeois wrote in one of her art pieces, "To unravel a torment, you must begin somewhere."[14] And poems, though perhaps not always torments, sometimes raucous yawps (in the case of Walt Whitman), or joyful expressions of being alive or noticing, all start somewhere. And I suggest that they always begin with a single word.

Since October 2020, I've been sending a weekly newsletter that offers the structure of a poem: a prompt with lines started for you, seven lines themed seasonally. (As I write this manuscript, I have sent 223 prompts, and I haven't missed a Monday yet.)

One of the joys of my work is seeing how people take these poetry vessels, the shape of these poems, and pour their own words, perspectives, and magic into them. Books have been written from these prompts. They have been brought to the ceremonies and rituals of other groups. They have been taken into classrooms, published in partnership with other newsletters and writers. They have taken on an amazing spiraling journey of their own. I am so grateful. My favorite kind of email to receive is a poem. Below, I have included some poem vessels based on each season to help inspire you to get started, as well as a finished poem that may show you what it might ultimately look like.

Once you begin to understand the poetic line and the impulse of finishing a line started for you, you might try to make your own prompts and see where the journey takes you. Much like Hansel and Gretel following their breadcrumbs through the forest, this might be the beginning of your poetry journey.

As I always share in the newsletter, there is no right or wrong way to do this. *The most important part is that you do.*

·•☽ Seven-Line Poetry Prompts ☾•·

For Spring

The Title: "A Horizon ____________"

Line 1: "I wait ______________________________"
Line 2: "The dark ____________________________"
Line 3: "A spring ____________________________"
Line 4: "There is _____________________________"
Line 5: "Water ______________________________"
Line 6: "Crafts ______________________________"
Line 7: "And there ___________________________"

A Horizon, Spring Arrives in the East

I wait at the threshold
of this season, the dark brings
balance. What some might call
the shadows, I call my
beloved self. A spring bursts forth
from the clouds,
the rains of this cycle.
There are seeds underfoot
they have been sleeping.
The water in the mud
crafts rivers, veins, lifeblood
of this planet. And there,
I am crying, standing in a field,
but I do not know the
difference between tears
and this wonderful rain

For Summer

The Title: "Summer ____________"

Line 1: "Spiral ______________________________"
Line 2: "Standing stones ______________________"

Line 3: "Sun ______________________________"
Line 4: "Changing __________________________"
Line 5: "Chthonic __________________________"
Line 6: "Kin ______________________________"
Line 7: "Summer ___________________________"

Summer Is a Spiral, as Most Things Are

Spiral season, standing stones,
sun glinting
through each window.
I am changing all the time.
Chthonic woman, I am
of the earth, breaking
up the soil to bloom.
Kin, of the world,
summer draws you closer
to me, each blade of grass
is an old friend.

For Autumn

The Title: "Equal ____________"

Line 1: "Night _____________________________"
Line 2: "Day ______________________________"

Line 3: "A shadow ____________________"
Line 4: "A blessing ____________________"
Line 5: "The seasons ____________________"
Line 6: "Soil ____________________"
Line 7: "Here ____________________"

Equal Shadow That Casts Itself Across the Land

Night falls as a prayer. Day balanced as its partner.
This is a shadow of longing, a blessing of the seasons.
Here, earth, take my joy and my grief as your own
to make good soil. Here, earth, we are the same. Both
seed collected and decay, an equinox.

For Winter

The Title: "Woven, the season ____________"

Line 1: "Here, possibility ____________________"
Line 2: "I remember ____________________"
Line 3: "The shadows ____________________"
Line 4: "The candle ____________________"
Line 5: "Threads ____________________"
Line 6: "Of my ____________________"
Line 7: "Winter ____________________"

Woven, the Season of Solstice Offers Threads

Here, possibility is like a spider. I remember the rituals of my youth, meeting with the shadows of this season. The candles in the window of my heart remember the threads given to me by my grandmothers in my dreams, remembered. Winter is a web, a lesson of togetherness, here, pull on this thread, and I'll weave with you.

·•☽ Songs of the Earth ☾•·

There is a famous quote (attributed to both Shakespeare and George Santayana) that says, "The Earth has music for those who listen." One of my favorites of these songs is the one I hear in spring. It is a gentle hum under the feet, which I like to imagine is from the billions of alive particles that make up the soil. A song can capture the heart, act as an anthem, and instill hope, but above all else, it makes us *feel* something.

I once sat in a room of fellow poets, led by poet and professor Aracelis Girmay. She told us to raise our hands when the music made us feel something, and then she put on "Que Sera, Sera" by Sly and the Family Stone. As the music cascaded and crescendoed, as the vocalists took turns singing, as the chorus of voices chimed in—I watched writers put their hands up one by one, tentatively at first and then more readily as the song went on. It was a wave of hands, an orchestra of feelings. Different parts of the music touched something deep inside us that made us react, and in turn, our hearts sang back. This moment has stayed with me ever since, because it was a visual representation of how music makes us feel.[15]

For centuries, humans have sung, played instruments, and gathered together in sacred places to chant, to channel, and to connect with the divine. Humans sing to the earth and the earth sings back. We don't just send our music into the void; the earth hears our songs and returns them with an expression of her own music.

Whenever we sing in the car, hum to ourselves, tap our foot, or drum against the dashboard or our desk, we're connecting with the human tradition and love of music. Songs get stuck in our head and provide a soundtrack to our days. We go to concerts and dance with hundreds and sometimes thousands of others—*all for the love of song.*

Many of these songs also have lyrics that stay with us, that we memorize, that haunt our hearts. Think of a line from a song you love. Can you pause for a moment and sing it to yourself? Why do you love the lyrics? What do the words make you feel or remember?

✸ *Language has music. Word Witches sing.* ✸

Poet and lecturer on the craft of writing Gregory Orr said about the musical temperament of the writer, "The musical temperament manifests itself in the individual qualities of syllables, in syntax, and assorted sound effects as they interact to create the poem's aural and rhythmical structure. Music in poetry is irrational; it works directly on the emotions, regardless of the purported content in the language. Primitive and powerful."[16]

Music is the rhythm, heartbeat, driving force, or undercurrent in writing, pushing the words along. Music is about the sound of the piece and the words. How does it feel in the body—a drumbeat, heartbeat, or song?

•●○●•

Once, I was participating in a ritual, and a fledgling song came to me out of nowhere. When the guide from the ritual paused to give us a break, I scrawled the song in my notebook as quickly as I could. It was only a handful of lines, accompanied by what could be called a chorus, refrain, or chant. Though music had always played a special role in my life, and I'd studied music in middle and high school (the piano and the cello) and spent a few years dabbling with the ukulele, I never really thought of myself as a musician—or even someone who was especially proficient in music. Even so, when I got home later, I revisited the song and started to see where it wanted to go. I moved a few words around, and finally, alone in my apartment, I sang it to life.

A Stand of Pines

Across the field I find, across the field I find
a stand of pines, a stand of pines, across the field, I find
a stand of pines, a stand of pines.

This voice is mine. This voice is mine. The song we carried together here. The song we carried together here.

The river runs clear. The water runs clear.

My wild is a stand of pines. My wild is a stand of pines.
This voice is mine. This voice is mine.

The song we carried together here. The river runs clear,
the water runs clear. The river made me smoothed, a stone.
In the forest, I'm never alone. The river made
me different, a stone.
In the forest, I'm never alone.

And so together we sing, our voices in an enchanted ring.
And so together we sing, our voices in an enchanted ring.

Across the field, I find, across the field I find,
a stand of pines
a stand of pines. Across the field, I find. A stand of
pines, a stand of pines.

Now, dear Word Witch, wherever you are in the world, whether you consider yourself to be a music maker or not, I want you to try to sing your version of this song. If you must start with a whisper, that's okay. Sing to the pine trees. Imagine all our voices together in a chorus. Imagine the words taking flight, and feel your throat, lungs, and heart unfurl.

Sing the song that is in *your* heart. The notes don't matter; getting it "right" doesn't matter. What matters is that you are connecting with your inner creative impulse for song, one that is healing and ancient. After you sing this piece, you might try your hand at creating lyrics or singing a song. Singing over a meal or while you cook is a beautiful way to add enchantment. Drumming with your poems can be a gorgeous way to connect with the heartbeat of your piece and all the people who have drummed before you. To sing is an expression of being alive. Sing to your altar, and hear it sing in return.

✸ *When we sing together, we are casting a spell.* ✸

Incorporating Music into Your Writing

There are many ways to incorporate music, song, and rhythm into your writing. In poetry, specifically, meter, rhyme, and sound play a big role in the finished composition.

Meter (etymologically related to the word "measure") contributes to the structure of a poetic line, consisting of two elements, both the number of syllables and the way that emphasis creates a pattern within the syllables. Rhyme helps create the rhythm structure of the poem, and there are many different rhyme schemes you can experiment with; this diversity is especially helpful when you're crafting spells. Sound makes its way into your writing through the alliteration, assonance, and consonance of the words themselves. Discovering how to use these tools together and wield language with intention allows you to make your writing sing.

Poetry Witch Annie Finch has done incredible work in the area of meter and poetry and their direct relationship to ritual and magic. In her incredible gift of a book, *How to Scan a Poem: A Poetry Witch Workbook,* she walks you through scansion, an important and yet often overlooked skill in contemporary poetry, and how to discover and listen to this music. She writes, "In fact the words 'meter' and 'magic' both spring from the same proto-Indo-European root, *meh meaning 'power.' During an era when meter helped poets to memorize the epics, legends, and healing and spiritual inheritance of their people, which otherwise would have been lost entirely, it is no wonder meter was regarded as magic and poets as direct channels to divine power."[17] The magic is in the meter, in the music of the words.

Writers have been singers and poets for as long as songwriting has been a practice. Those who write songs *are* Word Witches. Consider the work of Joni Mitchell, Bob Dylan, or Ramblin' Jack Elliott. These are three lyrically minded folk singers with beautiful storytelling skills and a gift for Word Witchery. They conjure and they create. *These are Word Witches at work!*

And those who are poets often use music to help them communicate their emotions in a given work. Whenever I've seen poet laureate Joy Harjo read, she has sung her pieces aloud. Videos of her readings are widely available on the internet, and I highly recommend you listen to them for yourself. I also think of the work of poet Anne Waldman, who has also incorporated music into her work, especially in *Fast Speaking Woman,* inspired by the mushroom chants of Maria Sabina.[18]

A great poem to listen to is "We Real Cool," written and performed by Gwendolyn Brooks.[19] Read aloud in her voice, with the power of enjambment, framed by storytelling, the poem has an engine; it has a heart; it becomes a song without even needing to be sung.

The Word Witch as Earth Steward

Earth-based connection and care, poetry, and songs are all revolutionary tools. Meaning, they create change. The earth needs all of us. I mean this because as I write this, many people who sit in places of power do not prioritize the care of our planet. Witchcraft and writing are forms of activism. Writing changes minds. Writing is a rallying cry. Writing is a way to share ideas, hope, inspiration, and to create a protective circle, a spell of shared intent. Writing is a form of resistance because it gives voice to the collective and the people. Writing is a spell of resilience because it is a way to celebrate being alive. Witches who honor and care for the earth must do so in radical ways. I cannot sit here and tell you to love that which we come from and not advise us all to fight for it, to stand up. Poet Dana Levin says it like this: "If you're a writer, you must write. Writing in resistance to the State is one kind of activism; writing about anything else is another. You don't know what might spark a helping change in someone, even if that change lasts only a second—what might meet a reader's fear or grief or rage or confusion and witness it. Ameliorate it. It might be a poem about snow or shoes or the confessing mirror. Poetry is an endurance technology."[20]

In a world that profits from our insecurity, of us being quiet and small, writing and sharing our stories is a radical act. When you are empowered to tell the truth of your life, you empower others to do the same. It's important who you read, read a variety of voices, from a variety of places and experiences. And through these portals, you will understand others better. The writer and the Word Witch have long been members of the archetype of activist or advocate. I urge you to use the practice of writing to stand up for what is right and just. I urge you to read the writing of those who have different experiences from you and those whose experiences validate your own. I urge you to learn and expand through new ways of seeing. I encourage you to be wrong. I encourage you to seek the fringe and the liminal, for we know that's where the Word Witch lives.

The earth is the home of the Word Witch.
✸ *The Word Witch knows we must be stewards* ✸
of this magical and mysterious place.

Journaling Prompts for Your Word Witch Journal

1. What symbols in nature remind you of the element of earth?
2. What did you discover by jotting down notes of things that inspired you through your rituals of paying attention?
3. Write a piece that "voices the natural," inspired by *The Wild Iris*.
4. How did it feel to write a seven-line poem?
5. How did it feel to sing along in "A Stand of Pines"?
6. Who are three lyricists that you see as Word Witches and why? What do you feel when you listen to their music? Allow their songs to inspire three different pieces of writing.
7. Do you commit to care for the earth and to be a steward of earth in your Word Witch practice? Write your commitment.

Chapter Eight

SPIRIT

Ancestors, Offerings, Bones, Thresholds, Veils, and Dreams

The Spirit Element

Direction: the below, the above, and the center
Symbolic Magic: the ancestors, the altar, offerings
Associations: veil, liminal, dreams, crossroads, thresholds
Ritual: pantheon of creative ancestors, leaving an offering, grief, thresholds

Your altar is now built. As you turned the pages of this book, you carefully crafted and connected the foundation with the four elements, honoring the wheel and bringing air, fire, water, and earth to the space. Through this spiral, you set your intentions, ritualized your writing, celebrated the cycles, and found new practices for your creative life. And now, you arrive at your altar with your writing practice, a Word Witch.

You can trust that all you have built and put your time and energy into can feed you reciprocally. You now know that you can surrender to the creative process and that the words will appear; all you must do is show up again and again. This is a writing life. I have been told, wisely, that persistence is the most essential skill of the Word Witch and writer. So, let me impart this wisdom to you: *Do not give up.*

The Word Witch turns to the altar
and the page again and again.

But as we arrive at the end of our journey, ready to venture out into the world as Word Witches, guided by our intuition and all we have practiced together here, there is one more threshold to cross. We have been waiting to weave in the fifth and final element: the element of spirit.

Spirit is the below, the above, and the center of our spiral; it is the nebulous, etheric other world we can't quite grasp with our hands. Spirit connects us, reminding us that life itself is a creative impulse. Some practitioners believe that the fifth element of spirit is the combination of the four elements that have come before it, while others believe it is the foundation, allowing the other four to be possible. To me, spirit is both before and after; spirit exists outside of definition, which is why it is our final stop on this spiral of the creative practice.

Spirit is the old stories, the symbolic serpents that represent creativity. Spirit is the offering that we bring to the altar, and spirit is the empty hands; spirit is the bones that live in our body, connecting us physically with our ancestors, but also the metaphorical bones, the bones of all that have come before us, the bones of the ancients and the storytellers. Spirit is the veil that separates this world from the next, the ancestors' whispers, the altar itself. Spirit is dreams, the murky dark of the subconscious that offers itself to us each night, creating and conjuring stories and symbols that we can retrieve into our waking life. To commune with the element of spirit is to commune with the creative spirit. They are cut from the same cloth. They are the threads of the same fabric.

✸ *To write with spirit, is to write as a Word Witch.* ✸

Spirit is the magic that will keep you writing, In the book *The Four Elements of the Wise: Working with Magickal Power of Earth, Air, Water, Fire,* as quoted in Taschen's Library of Esoterica *Witchcraft,* Ivo Dominguez Jr. describes the fifth element as "the fascia, mycelial network, the web, and the weft and warp of creation."[1]

Spirit is the animating force, the soul. I once had a creative writing teacher who told us not to worry about what we would "do" in the world because we studied stories, the language of this soul. She said there is no more important study than the human experience. I now know this to be true in my spirit bones. Stories have fed me; they created a lantern when I could not see the way, and they brought me back to myself again and again. Stories make the map. They are the map itself. Stories are the web and the weft.

✸ *Spirit is the altar; the altar is spirit.* ✸

Honoring the spirit honors the soul that houses our dreams, passions, grief, and struggles. The soul is worth listening to, always. The creative practice that you have made is alive. To write in this world, to make in this world is not a passive process; it is a human act, one of living fully and authentically. And that's precisely who the Word Witch is—your true self. To quote beloved nineties icon Angela Chase in *My So-Called Life*, "People always say you should be yourself, like yourself is this definite thing, like a toaster or something."[2] When I say "true self," I mean the non-definite. I mean the self that is always moving through the cycles of life. The authentic self is constantly shape-shifting and changing, which is part of the magic. Each facet of us is magic. This is the gift of the element of spirit.

To work with this constantly vanishing and amorphous idea, we can assign the element of spirit concrete symbols, crafted from our physical world, again, calling on the power of symbolic action. Spirit is symbolized and worked with in a ritual practice by calling upon the ancestors, bringing an offering at the altar, and working with the threshold, the veil, and the liminal spaces that exist everywhere.

The Ancestors

Much of the work of a Word Witch brings the magic maker back to the ancestors.

"Ancestor" can refer to many people beyond just your grandparents or even your grandparents' grandparents. From a bird's-eye view, the ancestors all had to come together so that you could now walk the earth. Ancestors can be guides, and they can be teachers. Ancestors can be of a family lineage or a larger cultural landscape. Ancestors can be stories, photographs, or your reflection in the mirror. When you look at your reflection, many people gaze back. (Look for them in your smile, eyes, freckles, and height.)

I never met my mother's mother, but I like to think about how we're both the tallest women in our families. I know I got my stature from her. The first poem I ever won an award for was a poem I wrote in 2005 when I was in the sixth grade. I remember it was displayed in the window of the framing shop in my hometown after it won. It goes like this…

Self-Portrait

Like a faded picture she stands there outside
She stands by a building worn out in my mind
Her smile is faded her thoughts I can't see
Could this girl be an old picture of me?
A part I've forgotten a part I don't know

Please don't leave me please don't go
She stands in her picture her thoughts I can't see
When I look at her I see me
She nods her head and smiles back
She knows what I know I understand that.

This piece was about seeing a photo of my grandmother I've never met. The poem and the photo are now framed together in the hallway at my mom's house. Ancestors can speak to us in all different kinds of ways and in all different types of places.

You might have known these ancestors personally while they were here, sharing space and lives together, or you might have connected with them solely through stories shared and passed down to you. I like to think about how these stories change over time. Eventually, our family members become myths themselves. They remain tethered to us through the power of storytelling and memory. The oral tradition of storytelling exists within our families, too, not just as a broad idea about where stories come from.

While many positively associate with their ancestors, this word can also raise questions about identity to varying degrees. For many reasons, you might not know who your ancestors are, and bloodlines can be obscured by the shadows of time. And not all our ancestors may resonate with us, or us with them. Still, I know that for every ancestor who might not have understood me while they were on this planet, there is one out there in the ether who may have been a Word Witch, healer, or wild woman, just like me. I do my work for them. This is why I call upon "the benevolent ancestors" when I invoke these spirits. I know I come from a long line of wild and wonderful humans, and I suspect, dear reader, you do, too.

I also like to think that death changes a spirit. I suspect some of my beloved dead have changed their minds over the years, and I always like to acknowledge this power of changing one's mind. I imagine that two hundred years from now, if I am gazing at my descendants through the veil, I may have different opinions than I do now. *And isn't that magic?* From where our ancestors now rest, they know and love us as we are. You can feel into this for yourself and make your own beliefs.

Spirit is not about knowing, it's about developing a relationship to belief and faith. *Spirit is about trust.* We must be guided by our hearts, our intuition, and the messages we get from spirit.

If you haven't already, there are many ways to connect with your ancestors. Consider turning to DNA tests and connecting with the stories of your genetics. You could also tune in to the ancestors of the land where you live and honor them as the caretakers and stewards of the ground where you walk and hopefully tend also. Or you could cook the food of the places and the people you have never met, turning over their spices and recipes in your hand, weaving and winding your way back through one of the most unifying things in the human experience, a meal.

Beyond our familial ancestors, we all have creative ancestors who paved the way for the work we do now and the words we share. As my dad, Kevin Belew, always reminds me, "You stand on the shoulders of those who came before you."

Creative Ancestors

It's important to remember that as Word Witches, writers are our ancestors, too. Those who wrote their stories created artifacts that can be later opened and revisited, and their novels, songs, and poetry are now altars. Hold any old book in your hands and feel the power that comes from that. I'll never forget visiting Atlantis Books in Santorini, Greece, at night just before close. Descending the stairs into the cavernous shop, walls filled with quotations and new and old books, I saw the Langs' Fairy Books. These colorful books lined the shelves of my grandparents' and mom's house growing up. So, when I walked straight up to the collection of hardbound, gold-embossed, line-illustrated books from the early 1900s, the shopkeeper, who happened to be from Memphis, told me I could pick any color I liked for twenty dollars. I held *The Olive Fairy Book* in my hands and felt every person who had held it before me and was connected back to my grandparents, who had also owned a copy. I was holding a magical artifact in our modern-day world.

An old book embodies the element of spirit. Stories are our ancestors; myths are our ancestors. We can turn to them to better understand where we came from and where we're going. When we peer into the past, stories are what have been handed down. In between the lines of the story, spells are whispered, lessons are transmuted, and healing has been enveloped into the words. When we create stories, we are good ancestors for those who come after us. When we pass down the stories we have learned and studied, we create an ancestral bridge between the generations of Word Witches. Stories are what make us human and tie us together. They are a part of the element of spirit because they make up those threads that we spoke about; they are the mycelial network itself.

Honoring the works of those who came before you is essential to your work as a Word Witch. As a part of your creative altar, I'd like you to add a representation of your creative ancestors to weave in this element of spirit.

As I reach out to you across this page, you must grab my hand but also turn around to hold the hand of the writer behind you. *This is how we create this web and chain.*

Even when origin stories are mixed messages, recorded in unreadable handwriting, or hardly remembered, they exist somewhere in our shared and collective history, in our DNA, in how we speak to each other, even when these myths are shaped by time, moldable clay.

If you need inspiration for your patron saints or pantheon (our next ritual for connecting with Spirit in our creative practice), consider the first author, Enheduanna. Though many have been writing, casting spells, and telling stories for as long as humans have been on this planet, the name of one Word Witch survives the erosion of time, and her name is Enheduanna. She was found again in 1927, after many years of dormant sleep, when archaeologist Sir Leonard Woolley uncovered objects inscribed with her name, which means "High Priestess, Ornament of Heaven" in Sumerian.

Enheduanna wrote forty-three hundred years ago in Mesopotamia. Many consider her the first recorded author, writing fifteen hundred years before Homer, seventeen hundred years before Sappho, and two thousand years before Aristotle (to add a bit of context!).

She was the daughter of the Akkadian founder, Sargon the Great, a king who made her the high priestess of the most highly regarded temple in Sumer. Through poems, prayers, and blessings, she shaped how humans conversed with the gods. *She was a channel for the divine.*

Her writings, particularly, were in conversation, admiration, and veneration of the goddess Inanna. Inanna is known mythically for her famous descent into the underworld, and then her ascension. She is a goddess of initiation. Our beloved ancestral Word Witch is remembered now for her works "Inninsagurra," "Ninmesarra," and "Inninmehusa," which translate as "The Great-Hearted Mistress," "The Exaltation of Inanna," and "Goddess of the Fearsome Divine Powers," all three hymns to the goddess Inanna.[3]

In this prose from her poem "The Exaltation of Inanna," she describes the creative process:

I have given birth,
Oh exalted lady, (to this song) for you.
That which I recited to you at (mid)night
May the singer repeat it to you at noon![4]

Of course, her claim to this title of first author is contested, as many things this old are, but historians who have examined the discs, the remembered writings, and her work say otherwise.

Jungian analyst and Enheduanna translator Betty De Shong Meador, writes in her 2009 book, *Princess, Priestess, Poet,* "The voice we hear in the hymns is that of a gifted poet. She describes with candour the everyday lives, cares, and inherent nature of the deities and their temples. She populates the entire surrounding cosmos with active, engaging, uncontrollable divine beings."[5]

Through the winding caverns of history, Enheduanna's name still appears on the page, and her relationship with the great goddess still prevails and inspires.

One of the most sacred things a Word Witch can do is to look at the web in which they create (*in which we create*). We make in the lineage of—both extending a hand backward and forward, whispering these poems, scraps of prose back and forth. The sacredness of language is a language itself. History informs our future.

The Word Witch knows that the creativity
of others gives us creativity in return.
All in reciprocity, magic.

So, if you ever find yourself at the altar of your page, feeling lost, fearful, or in prayer, look to the great Word Witches of the past, and remember that somewhere, in another time, a woman wrote:

"I took up my place in the sanctuary dwelling, / I was high priestess, I, Enheduanna."

Another Word Witch who reaches from the past through the page is poet John Keats. I am often reminded of the poem

"This Living Hand," which he crafted just shortly before he stopped writing and just over a year before dying of tuberculosis at the young age of twenty-five, in an apartment overlooking the Spanish Steps in Rome. Keats understood the inherent play of the spirit world at the heart of making and writing.

This living hand, now warm and capable
Of earnest grasping, would, if it were cold
And in the icy silence of the tomb,
So haunt thy days and chill thy dreaming nights
That thou would wish thine own heart dry of blood
So in my veins red life might stream again,
And thou be conscience-calmed—see here it is—
I hold it towards you.[6]

In his poem, he reaches across the past, gesturing to the reader, "Yes, I am now alive, but someday I won't be, and yet this hand will continue to reach." Isn't it strange how the act of writing can transcend our own lives? By reading, we are listening to the ancestors, like Keats, and by writing, we ourselves are creating ancestral magic that we can hand down. We need to do both: listen and transmute. We must grab Keats's hand and yet also reach. *Storytelling flows both ways in time.*

Adding Your Pantheon of Witches and Writers to Your Word Witch Altar

One of your ritual offerings in this chapter is to consider your patron saints, your pantheon of Witches and writers. As you write, imagine, and know that you are a part of a vast web; you might call this the Witch Wide Web (a term I coined alongside my *Magick & Alchemy* cohost Kristin Lisenby). This web extends back to the first writer and storyteller and as far forward as all the writers and Word Witches who will come after you. Ask yourself: "Who do I write in the lineage *of* and *for*?"

Maybe your great-aunt was an author. Maybe you dream of teaching your grandchildren poetry, or perhaps you write for Emily Dickinson, Sappho, Sylvia Plath, or Lucille Clifton. Though writing is a solitary act, it's important to remember that we never write alone. We write alongside all the other writers in history who have put pen to page. We write and speak for our communities and our families. We share our ideas; our ideas are shared. Though we may physically write in a space by ourselves, those ancestral past, present, and future Word Witches accompany us in spirit.

This ritual honors those you write in the lineage of and whose work will continue to inspire you on your Word Witch path. To do so, you must first visit the altar of your bookshelf, library, or computer and consider who your creative ancestors are.

These are the writers whose words whisper to you even from beyond the grave. They are the writers who said the hard thing, inspired you to write, and made you gasp, laugh, or cry as you read their work. They are the ones whose words you pinned on your wall or copied down into your notebook. They are part of the collage of what makes you, you. They wrote so that *you* could write. They were timely and yet timeless. They made work that spoke to the systems and the world they lived in, yet they continue to speak to younger generations.

Now pick three creative ancestors that you'd like to honor. Write down their names and why their work is essential to you in your Word Witch journal.

Next you'll need a physical representation of each of them or their words. You can print a photo of them from the internet, paint or draw your interpretation of their likeness, or even copy down a quote from one of your favorite works by them on a piece of paper.

Then add these three guides, creative deities, allies, and Word Witches to your altar. There they'll remind you that you create from a wild and wyrd and knowing web, that you write and make so that those who come after you can write and make. You can call upon them when writer's block comes knocking or you lose connection to your work.

Some practical ways to work with these creative ancestors can be to create an automatic writing ritual as we did in the fire element chapter, but this time to receive advice or messages from these spirits. You can write letters to them and ask for a response in your dreams (which we'll discuss more in a moment). You can also imagine how they might respond to a creative problem that you're facing, or work with their writing to practice bibliomancy, asking their words to show you a way forward, a spark of inspiration, or a way through.

Simple Steps for Practicing Bibliomancy

1. Select a book by one of your creative ancestors (or a book that resonates with you magically).
2. Set an intention for your practice. For example, "I intend to receive a message by divining with this book of my creative ancestor."
3. Write a question in your Word Witch journal. For example, "Can you please give me the first line of this piece of writing?" or "What would you like to share with me about the writing process?"
4. Flip through the pages of the book until you feel the intuitive impulse to stop.
5. Place your finger somewhere on your page and receive your message.
6. Write the response in your Word Witch journal next to your question (don't forget to write down the book and the page number in case you'd like to return!).

The Ancestors

In addition to your creative ancestor pantheon on your altar, I invite you to add an ancestral item from your lineage. It can be dirt from the earth if you want to honor the collective ancestor of humanity, who have been returned to the earth. You can include a photo of your great-grandmother no longer in her human form, a pocket watch from a great-grandfather, a recipe card in your mom's handwriting if she's no longer with you, or even just a picture of where your DNA results show that you come from. For example, a few items on my altar are a woodblock carved by my Grandma Joyce, a book of poems with her handwriting in between the lines, and a depiction of Mary from my Grandma Joan's house.

The stories of our ancestors and genetics are constantly evolving. There is always more to learn and listen to. When I did my genetic research, I discovered on 23andMe that I share an ancient maternal line with a woman now named Ava who lived in prehistoric Scotland. She lived and died about 4,250 years ago, and she was found again in 1987. She was buried there in her resting place with a beaker of oats and barley, heather, buttercups, and meadowsweet, along with flint and a cow scapula.

I like to think of her and her cow scapula. She exists so far in the past that I'll never be able to know what she looked like, and I still wonder if any of my features resemble hers. But for me to live, *she* had to live, with her heather, buttercups, and meadowsweet. Someday I'll build an altar for this woman, with a cow scapula and porridge, to say hello to her spirit wherever it is. Someday maybe I'll even travel to Scotland.

There are so many branches of a family tree, so explore your own, one branch at a time. This is the practice of a lifetime. We make magic when we celebrate and honor, giving attention to each root, piece of bark, branch, and leaf. We are all connected to our trees, and together, how beautiful it is that we create a forest of stories. As you place your chosen ancestral item on your Word Witch altar, close your eyes, and thank all who came before you, who support you now on your creative and magical journey. Much like you might turn to your creative ancestors, you can also reach out to your familial ancestors for support. I have found great success asking for specific help from those beyond the veil. *Just make sure you bring an offering.*

The Offering and the Altar

An offering is something given or sacrificed to the gods or the divine at the altar. An offering is presented from a humble place, a kneeling place. It is a form of connection, a ritual for speaking with life, the force that animates us all, as well as the ancestors and the benevolent spirits. It's a way to communicate and thank them for their protection, guidance, and presence.

Offerings are a way to collaborate with your altar and co-create. As you can see from the previous chapters, creating an altar for creativity and creating a creative writing practice are not passive ventures. They require generosity, respect, curiosity, and attention.

Offerings can be many kinds of things. I have offered oils, herbs, smoke, candles, prayers, blessings, poems, tears, hair, stones, and crystals, to name a few. I have also offered goblets of wine, corn bread, inscribed books, cigarettes, hatpins, and typewriter poems; the options and possibilities are as endless as your expressions of love and dedication. An offering doesn't have to be perfect, either. The most important part of an offering is that it is sincere—of you, by you, offered with intention. It is something given from your heart that you value and hold close. Just making the offering itself is *always enough.*

Offerings can be tangible, like donations made in the name of a beloved dead, or more elusive, like a whisper of remembrance over an altar. They can be small, like a bit of water in a dish, or large, like a statue to honor a deity carved from stone.

Ritual:
Crafting an Elegy

One of the most sacred things we can offer is our grief. Grief can be a powerful impetus for both writing and Word Witchery, and writing can help alchemize grief. Our grief can also be an offering on its own, and the earth is here to support us.

Grieving is a genuine outpouring of emotion and expression. It is vulnerability in its pure form. In *The Flowering Wand,* author Sophie Strand shares, "Each death opens up a wound, and a song."[7] I would add to this that each death also opens a poem or a story.

As a Word Witch I have stood in front of funerals, sat beside grievers, and attended graveside as a mourner, but also as a poet, writer, and a magic maker. I have worked with spouses to craft dedications and odes to their beloved gone. And through these words, something is remembered. Spirit is conjured up, and healing is made possible. Poems and songs are medicine from the earth for our offerings of grief; they weave together on the spiral.

These expressions of grief made sacred are from the humble human heart, a gift. Through words, this grief finds new pathways, allowing a different story to be told. Grief magic is found through singing and poetry. It is an offering of being human. In *Grief Spells with Mara June,* Mara compares the griever to the Major Arcana tarot archetype of the Magician, one who works with enchantment, saying, "In grief, we learn to bear unbearable feelings alongside feelings of love and awe. Perhaps the magician is the wisdom of our animal bodies that allows us to be both ruined and blooming."[8]

During deep mourning, I have turned to poetry, specifically elegy, to process my grief. An elegy is a poetic form that creates a vessel for grieving. It is a lament for the dead. An elegy allows for the lines of writing to hold sorrow; it mourns the dead, and it also allows for metaphor; it creates a landscape for the loss. Much like funeral lamentations, wailing, or keening, the elegy lets out a gasp, a cry, or allows the tears to fall, transmuted through the page. Creating an elegy, arriving at the page and the altar with your grief, is a beautiful offering to spirit and can be done at any time in your creative practice.

There have been many famous elegies by authors of the classics, including "Adonais: An Elegy on the Death of John Keats" by Percy Bysshe Shelley; "Lycidas" by John Milton; "In Memoriam" by Alfred, Lord Tennyson; "When Lilacs Last in the Dooryard Bloom'd" by Walt Whitman; *Duino Elegies* by Rainer Maria Rilke; "O Captain! My Captain!" by Walt Whitman, and "Fugue of Death" by Paul Celan. Contemporary examples include "Elegy" by Aracelis Girmay and "Elegy" by W. S. Merwin.

While there are more classic forms to create elegies from, I have made one for the Word Witches, inspired by the three main parts of a traditional elegy (sorrow, admiration, and solace), as a way to make an offering of grief to bring to your altar. Here is an example of a form, a vessel, to help hold your grief:

Three Parts of an Elegy: Sorrow, Admiration, Solace

Line One: Sorrow
Line Two: Sorrow
Line Three: Admiration
Line Four: Admiration
Line Five: Solace
Line Six: Solace

And an example:

An Elegy for Grandma Joan

Joan, I keep your voicemails on my phone.
I loved the way you drove through the country
side rescuing dogs with a large iced tea from
the Wounded Minnow in your cup holder. I know
I will see you in some other life. Maybe only
smoking a cigarette with you outside the bar,
sharing a piece of gossip or staring at the sky in silence.

After you complete your piece, you can read it aloud, tuck it into your Word Witch journal, or leave it as an offering at your altar. If you're able to share your piece of writing wherever the person is buried or a place where you feel particularly close to the person you have lost, this can be a beautiful ritual of grief magic in and of itself.

✸ *Word Witches know that grief is a sacred offering.* ✸

Ritual:
•☽ Make an Offering at Your Word Witch Altar ☾•

In this ritual, I invite you to visit your altar and share a silent meal or drink as an offering to your creativity. A variety of the dumb supper, a ritual practice where a silent meal is held with the intention of connecting with spirits from beyond the veil, this act of communing with your muses, inspiration, or your Word Witch self can be a way to tap into your subconscious and honor messages from your higher self.

As you prepare your meal or offering, think about the intentions you wish to weave into your altar making and creative practice. Prepare two plates in silence—one for you and one for your offering to place on the altar. When you've finished, take your Word Witch notebook and sit before your altar, placing the offering plate on the foundation among your vessel of water, candle, earth-given gift, and symbolic air. You might consider lighting the candle, too, if it feels right.

As you eat, consider what offerings feel most potent to you. Consider how you nourish your writing practice, as food nourishes your body. As you sit with your altar, you can either wait in silence, seeing what messages appear for you, or you can practice your automatic writing (ritual found in the fire chapter), letting the words stream free, without judgment, and see what messages appear among the channeled writing from your inner Word Witch. What does she/he/they/we want you to know about this journey and the path that has been appearing under your feet?

When building your creative practice, consider what other offerings feel right to you. Personally, I always keep a glass dish filled with water on my creative altar for any spirit that passes by that may want to share an idea or inspiration with me from a benevolent place. I enjoy refilling the dish once the water evaporates, a reminder to continue to fill the well that you draw from as you make again and again. A reminder that all things come in cycles. And like water, a reminder to find my own flow, my own deep well to draw my Word Witchery from.

Through spending time in silence at the altar, or making a meal as an offering, you might find a new connection with the space, one that nourishes. You could research the recipes of both your creative ancestors or your familial ancestors and see how the experiences differ. One time, during my undergraduate years, my poetry class made and enjoyed a cake from one of Emily Dickinson's recipes, and as we did, we felt her spirit draw close. *Experiment!* Allow the imperfect offering to continually connect you with that spiritual place.

The Bones and Empty Hands

Sometimes the Word Witch travels
to the altar empty-handed.

The altar is a two-way flow of energy, a structure to be poured into and a place to receive creative support. This is a place to communicate with the element of spirit, because it has been crafted lovingly by the rest of the spiral, of the elemental circle.

Remembering that part of the magic is reciprocity, balance, and divine harmony, as we explored with the earth element, is important. Magic is about giving and receiving, listening, witnessing, and creating. Along your creative journey, your altar has been listening to you and wants to return the exchange. You may feel doubt when you first appear with your empty hands before the page and the altar. Doubt is a natural part of the process, and in fact, it can be helpful. Doubt can lead to curiosity, exploration, and possibility. Doubt is the sand in the oyster, the nagging thing that creates the pearl—as long as you don't give in to it.

What they call "writer's block" is a natural part of the process. There can be many different reasons for why you resist your writing practice, struggle with the topic of a subject, or muse for what feels like weeks over the structure of a piece. But if we take a breath to pause our frustration and allow these moments of creative blocks to generate tension, we sometimes find they can be spells instead of curses. *This is the hands, open.*

And in the hands are the bones. Magically speaking, bone is not only the structure of the skeleton but also the innermost part of a person, their soul—they carry feelings, ancestry, story. There are twenty-seven bones in the human hand alone. Each bone connects the earthly body with the beyond. The bones hold the memories, the deep feelings, of the body. They give structure to the tissue. They are the constraints that allow the creativity within the human body to ebb and flow freely. Bones have also long been used in witchcraft and magic, and you might see the mindfully collected bones of our kin as representations to the otherworld, as protection, as guides upon our altars. Bones, much like the bones outside the house of Baba Yaga, who we met during the fire element chapter when we went to the crone to seek inspiration, are the gift of our ancestors. Turn to the bones when you're not sure where to go.

The bones are always with us. The guides from the beyond are ever present for the Word Witch.

Asking for help and support can be difficult for some, nearly impossible for others. The empty hands, in their way, represent an ask. When you go to the altar with your empty hands, palms open, ready to receive, you can expect to find the gifts of your altar waiting for you.

To feel this magic, place your hands or hand in front of you. Turn them upward toward the sky. And imagine that they're not empty at all but instead full of working and living and breathing magic. Much like praying, by bringing your hands together, you're channeling the energy.

In building the altar, your body has also built the creative process. Even when your practice or the process appears stalled, your empty hands instinctively know that more is at work below the surface. Beyond the metaphor, we also know this in our actual bodies, which can be a source of great magic. Although you might often feel like you're writing in isolation, you're writing with all of those in your creative communities and all of those spirits on your spiritual teams. And to access them, all you need to do is let them in.

A simple ritual to banish "writer's block" is to sit in front of your altar—the altar you've spent this book connecting with, building, actively listening to, and working with. Now is the time to ask for support. Call a circle, light the candle, and feel your creativity rise up within you as a living and breathing thing. You can ask the altar a question, such as "What do I need to know before I take on this creative project," or "What should I pay attention to in this practice," or "What would my creative ancestors like to share with me?" The possibilities are as endless as your curiosity, and know that you'll receive an answer.

There is no other road other than the way through. When you ask for help, and then listen and offer your attention to the guidance that comes, your words will flow again. The dominant culture wants you to believe that you must always be productive or creating, but often, creation comes from the void. The emptiness and stillness of all things. When you're in tune with the cycles and spirals of all things and you allow yourself to do truly *nothing*, you might be surprised about what you find.

The Duende

One of my favorite theories of inspiration is Federico Garcia Lorca's duende. I first heard about this mysterious and creative spirit from poet and professor Diane Seuss. I remember sitting in her office during office hours, fish bones hanging on the door, sipping coffee from what was a jalapeño jar in its previous life, and being deeply inspired by Lorca's words. I knew then I would study and love poems for the rest of my life, *guided by this spirit*.

Federico Garcia Lorca—a renowned poet, who was murdered by nationalists in Spain for his politics and for being a queer and outspoken artist—theorized that there are angels, and there are muses, and then there is the duende.

Duende has its roots in the folklore from Spain, Portugal, and parts of Mexico, related to the spirits of the house, the goblins, the elves. In a lecture titled "The Theory and Play of Duende," Lorca considered duende to be the "dark sounds" of a creative practice drawn from the muck of the earth. He contrasted duende with the muse and the angels. This theory suggests that inspiration from these celestial guardians comes from some heavenly force from above, while the duende comes from inside the writer themselves. The duende must be awakened, danced with, and summoned. I associate duende with the element of spirit, and the below, because of how Lorca writes that duende surges up through the soles of the feet.

Duende is about that wild expression, the intuitive nature of spirit, the creative impulse that we can't grasp, but instead constantly seek. The Word Witch engages with this mystery bravely, the unknown and the liminal are always a source of inspiration.

Musician Nick Cave has spoken about his relationship with the duende, saying that he believes that Bob Dylan has duende and Leonard Cohen works with this force. He says that the duende follows Van Morrison, it can be summoned by Tom Waits and Neil Young.[9] I'd like to add that Joni Mitchell knows the duende, and Janis Joplin was deeply connected to this spirit, as was Aretha Franklin.

This is the type of energy of the duende. Put on any of these musicians and you can hear the quivering soul, the capacity for sadness, that gives the work of art its deep connection with spirit.

To Lorca, the duende has a soul, an acceptance of death; it is haunted, ever present in the dancing of flamenco dancers, singers, and poets. That which has a capacity to understand death is somehow the most alive.

Lorca writes, "The duende . . . Where is the duende? Through the empty archway, a wind of the spirit enters, blowing insistently over the heads of the dead in search of new landscapes and unknown accents: a wind with the odor of a child's saliva, crushed grass, and medusa's veil announcing the endless baptism of freshly created things."[10]

The duende comes from the roots. In the flamenco competition described by Lorca, the duende is the old woman who walks to the stage, throws her cane down, stomps her foot, and wins the competition. Duende is a creative possession.

When writing, consider the duende, the spirit, to be an ally to you in your process. The duende is here to teach you about your relationship to inspiration. Inspiration is not some etheric thing, but rather a force, a conjuring, a figure of folklore and myth. When you long for inspiration in your Word Witch practice, connect to spirit. This spirit is one you can turn to, to connect with that innate magic felt in words that are from the earth. Care for the duende, and the duende will compel you forward, always tumbling toward the type of magic that encourages us to create.

✸ *The Word Witch dances with the duende.* ✸

Crossing a Threshold, Donning a Veil

The element of spirit is symbolically associated with the veil, the threshold, and the liminal. A liminal space is an in-between space. A place of flux. A place or transition, change, where two things meet. The word "liminal" comes from the Latin word *limen,* which means "threshold."

✸ *The Word Witch creates in the liminal.* ✸

The etymology of threshold comes from the word "threshing," which is the act of loosening or separating the edible part of grain from the straw and husk. It also comes from the word "entryway," a way through, a starting point. A threshold is a place that makes us different, separating one moment of life from another, a blessing, an initiation. Once you cross a threshold, there is no returning to the way things were in the before times, all is made different through the ritual of crossing that space.

In a quote attributed to poet William Blake, the writer said, "In the universe, there are things that are known, and things that are unknown, and in between them, there are doors." There are doors everywhere. A door opens, a door closes, one journey ends, another begins.

"The veil" between worlds is both a very old and a newer idea at the same time. The language for this veil "being thin" may have its roots in Victorian-era spiritualism; however, the otherworld, the realm of the ancestors, bardos, heavens, hells, and afterlives, is as old as the human spirit itself. And the symbol of the veil is similarly ancient. Many deities, like the Greek goddess Artemis, the Celtic crone the Cailleach, and the Egyptian goddess Isis, are veiled in their depiction. Brides on their wedding day don veils, to symbolize crossing a threshold; they are also seen at funerals, as mourners grieve behind the gauzy layer, as they say goodbye to loved ones, and mark their absence through the rites of funerals.[11]

The veil separates, but it also clings to. I am reminded of the word "cleaving," which simultaneously comes together and pulls apart, a word that was beloved in my poetry classes for its strange pull in opposites—the veil cleaves. The veil separates. The veil connects this world and the next.

In each stitch of the veil, magic is woven in. Ritualists have known this for centuries. Another word for story is "a yarn." One "spins a story," and one "weaves a tale." The origin of the word spinster refers to the spinner women, those who gathered over the weaving and told stories, passing on the Word Witchery from elder to new initiate. No veil was made without these spells and stories being stitched in. Word Witch Danielle Dulsky spins the magic of the spinster like this: "We weave a tale. We spin a yarn, and, in that hallowed space between the once-upon-a-time and the ever-after, we are contained within a hand-knit house of meaning, bound by a certain fate."[12]

The veil that separates us from the beyond today may be crafted with and by these stories themselves. Though there was not much left from my grandma's family in Poland, before my Grandma Joan died, she sent me a doily made by one of the women in her family, aunts, grandmothers, always stitching. She told me, laughing, "I think this thing is ugly, but I also feel you should have it," and mailed it anyway. Although she didn't have the exact story or memory from when the textile was crafted, she had the lace in her hands as artifact. The passing down of the woven lace, in a way, is the story. I will never know those ancestors, but I carry their handiwork. From beyond the veil, the spirit of the ancestors reaches; the spirit of the stories sings.

There are many places to find where this world connects with the otherworld and where the veil is thin: some suggest Samhain, from the cycles of the wheel of the year, or spring equinox, when the bones appear from beneath the snow; others suggest the roots of trees, especially the willow, a tree that straddles both land and water, suggesting their liminality.

Becoming familiar with this in-between place is the work of a Word Witch. Where the element of ether and spirit linger, betwixt and between. Liminal spaces can be found everywhere. A crossroads can be a liminal space, a train station, the subway, a corridor, a waiting room. The liminal is the place of the magic maker; it's the times of dusk and dawn, the cross-quarter days between seasons, and the place just before waking and falling asleep. Here in New York City, I find great inspiration in the liminal place of the subway. The subway is the crossroads. Sit on the train and look around: The creative spirits, the journeys of so many with dreams, spiral together before, like a leaf catching a wind, they take their leave and head out into their own lives.

If you don't live in a bustling city, your crossroads are still plentiful. Go anywhere where the paths of strangers cross (grocery stores, sidewalks in the center of town, a casino, a gas station parking lot), and you'll find a connection with the surreal and strange magic of liminality.

The thin, veiled, and the narrow places are places where spirit communes with us, your altar for example, and the page. Thresholds are also places where two things can be brought together. This is sometimes when, in an alchemical wedding ceremony the couple jumps over a broom together, symbolizing a threshold, or when someone is carried across the threshold of their new home. Crossing a threshold, through the liminal, is a powerful ritual.

The Word Witch communes with the strangeness of the thinly veiled threshold spaces, knowing that the spirit of creativity meets with them there.

Ritual: The Threshold

Now that we've connected to the etheric element of spirit, listened, and ritualized, we are nearing the end of our time together. This is a threshold in itself. As you close this book, you will step across the metaphorical threshold in your writing practice and take your magic into your next phase of writing. For one of our final rituals together, I invite you to imagine a symbolic threshold you're crossing in your life. A symbolic threshold is anything in your life that has a before and an after. Symbolic thresholds that work nicely for this ritual are birthdays, weddings, New Year's, births, and deaths, to name a few, and this ritual can be revisited at any of these crossroads. Today, imagine a threshold in your writing practice, your Word Witch journey.

As you imagine this threshold, this separation of before and after, I invite you to write a letter to the threshold. In your letter, honor whatever has passed. Acknowledge the before and after of this moment, grieve what longs to be grieved, note what the threshold means to you and what it symbolizes, and then cast your eyes to the other side of the threshold. What hopes, fears, anxieties, or intentions do you have for the days on the other side of the threshold? Then, finally, finish your letter with three blessings: *a blessing on what has passed, a blessing on the present and the threshold, and a blessing on the future* (if you need the format for a blessing, return to our air chapter).

After you finish your letter, I invite you to read your letter aloud and then take a step across, a leap, or a twirl over a physical threshold in your space. This can be a doorway, an entryway, a broom laid flat, a candle to jump over, a line in the sidewalk, anything. Revisit this threshold moment after a moon phase has passed (full moon to full moon or new moon to new moon), a season, or year from now, and reflect on what it meant to you to cross this liminal space. Let the spirit of the threshold work its magic in your writing life.

Dreams

Sometimes, when we can't open a book or sit with the empty page, we can also turn to our dreams for creative support. Dreams are another way to touch that liminal space in our life, to tap into the magic of spirit, the creative force.

Poet Alice Notley said, "We say that dreams, poems, and stories occur in the imagination, or the psyche, or whatever word we're using right now, to invent another entity that doesn't concretely exist to put them in. But doesn't the 'real world' exist in some collective category like that? All we do is dream; we live in poems and stories we invent."[13] Dreams are the deep well of consciousness that our brain works out every night, but every time we come to the page, we dream a dream of possibility.

Dreams have long fascinated humans, and many have spent much dedication and study to the work of dreams. Oneiromancy is a word that describes working with dreams for divination.[14] The ancient Sumerians in Mesopotamia left evidence of dream interpretation. The earliest vision, recorded on cuneiform was from 2700 BC.[15] Those who had many dreams were often considered blessed by the gods.

Every night, whether you remember it upon waking or not, you dream. Dreams are full of symbols, messages, surreal beauty, strangeness, and sometimes fear or confusion—but this extensive range is what makes them such helpful conduits for creativity. The symbols create the magic of symbolic action, after all. They conjure on the pages, allowing us to act as oracles.

Crafting a dream journal is one of the most potent ways to connect with your dreams and your intuition. This can be done by dedicating a journal, or space in your Word Witch journal, to your dreaming practice and putting it next to your bed. Before you go to sleep, you can write an intention statement like "Tonight I will remember my dreams" or "Tonight in my dreams I will see ____________."

Place the journal next to where you sleep, and when you wake up in the morning you can write the first thoughts of your day in there, even if it's "didn't recall" or "didn't remember." By paying attention and honoring this practice, your dreams may start to linger, offering you notes, symbols, and stories from your subconscious. Even the smallest or strangest detail can be the seed of a story. If you don't remember anything, record that, too. See what sparks of inspiration can be divined from this sacred sleeping place. The dream allows us to craft another threshold, another place to meet with spirit.

Ritual:
·•☽ Connecting with Spirit ☾•·

Word Witch, we have arrived at the final ritual on our path together. Together, we have traveled with the sacred spiral of our circle, we have connected to the four directions, to the below, the above, and now finally to the center of our practice. You were a Word Witch at the beginning of this journey, but how do you feel as a writer, now? I invite you one last time in our ritual to connect with spirit. Close your eyes in front of your altar and take three deep breaths. Picture all the magic channeled through this space, into your Word Witch journal, and all the threads, possibilities, and portals into your creative work that you have ventured through, the threshold you have stepped across. Think of all you have discovered through your words and yet how much is left to learn.

Word Witches are forever students, who seek to learn, understand, and love the world.

Look to spirit and your ancestors (both creative and otherwise); look to the earth, with your poems, witnessing, and song; look to the water, and honor the cycles and the tides of your creativity; look to the fire and celebrate play, and alchemical magic; look to the air, and remember the blessings, and connect with the oracles of birds. You have stitched a circle; you have written in the circle; you have practiced and built the life of a Word Witch.

Word Witch, I have an invitation for you. I want you to reflect on your altar-building experience, from the reclamation of your name to the intentions that you set. I want you to consider the symbols you chose and the words you were drawn to, which myths spoke to you, as if from the beyond, and what stories have appeared as lanterns on your path. And now that you've built this space in your life and on your altar, I want you to set a new intention. One for your life as a writer, as you close this book and venture off the page to tell new stories and craft new poems. In your Word Witch journal, I want you to put a seal on your experience that we had here together and say it as a spell.

Word Witch, you must write, you must share your stories, tell your truths, and be authentically you. Listen to the blank page, for it is full of spells of inspiration. Go outside, with your grief and your joy and your attention. Attend the ritual of being alive with radical presence. Write yourself onto your path.

Below is a template for the spell for your Word Witch life . . .

As I close this journey as a Word Witch, I begin my next adventure as a writer. I set my intention. I will ________. So mote it be or something better.

Once you set this intention, read it aloud. You are ready to continue your Word Witch path, and know that this book and its rituals will always be here for you to return to.

Continue to craft in your Word Witch journal, allow the rituals to lead you on the spiral path of writing. You can take down your altar, rebuild it, or leave it up and tend to it (leaving offerings and cultivating it as a space for your creativity). The magic is yours; it's ours; it's for all of us.

It's time to craft *your* writing world, Word Witch.

Journaling Prompts for Your Word Witch Journal

1. What symbols in nature or stories remind you of the element of spirit?
2. What has your altar taught you?
3. What intention or intentions would you like to set as you cross the threshold of our practices?
4. What does the word "ancestor" mean to you?
5. Reflect on your threshold ritual, what happened? What did you discover?
6. Read the lecture "The Theory and Play of Duende." What can this symbol of spirit in the creative process teach you?
7. What did you learn about offerings in your creative practice?
8. Dedicate a week to listening to messages from your dreams in your Word Witch journal.
9. As you come to the end of the spiral, how do you now see spirit, earth, water, fire, and air woven together in both your altar practice and your writing practice?
10. What does it mean to be a Word Witch?
11. What are your basic principles as a Word Witch? What do you commit to in your craft?

A FINAL BLESSING, FOR NOW

Let me now open the circle that we cast together in this book. At the end of the ritual, it's important to open the circle, to remember that the circle, though it opens, is never broken. *Thank you, to the spirit of the center. Thank you to the spirits of the above. Thank you to the spirits of the below. Thank you to the spirits of the earth in the north. Thank you to the spirits of the water in the west. Thank you to the spirits of the fire in the south. Thank you to the spirits of the air in the east. May the peace of the Goddess live forever in our hearts. Our circle is open yet unbroken. Merry meet, and merry part, merry meet, and merry part, merry meet, and merry part, and merry meet again.*

I have a parting blessing for you, Word Witch: Your writing will be messy. It will be full of mistakes, and it will rage against the facade of separateness and perfectionism—and it will be all yours. Your words will help you, guide you. They are lanterns on the path to this joy.

Your words are *your* words. Your heart is *your* heart. It beats in time with all the other hearts and speaks in language with all the languages. Allow your writing to take you on a journey, one that is authentic to you. Relish in the accomplishments that come; learn from the obstacles you encounter along the way. And for every hand extended to you, make sure to turn around and extend one, too. There is no doing this alone.

And as you walk the path of the Word Witch, Word Witchery will keep winding its web, casting its spell, and creating a magical life for you in its wake.

Your life will be magic because you are magical.
Your life will be full of writing because
you are a Word Witch.

ACKNOWLEDGMENTS

To the spirits of the air in the east, the fire in the south, the water in the west, the earth in the north, the below, the above, and the center, thank you for creating the circle from which this book was crafted.

This book is a spiral of all my experiences as someone who believes in the power of writing and magic. It would not be possible without the magic given to me through the love and support of others. To all of those who have supported me in this work, you know who you are and I'm so grateful to and for you.

Thank you to my husband, Cody, for the enchantment and magic you bring to our lives; you make this work possible. Thank you to my dog, Banjo, my constant familiar and soul companion.

Thank you to my sister, Grace, and my brother, Aidan, who have been with me on this path since the beginning, my always travelers. Thank you to my parents, Patty and Kevin. It's an honor, Mom, it's an honor, Dad, to be your daughter. Thank you to my stepdad, Kelly. Thank you to my stepmom, Honor.

Thank you to Grandma Joan, Grandpa Ken, Pop Pop, Grandma Joyce, Grandma Lucy, Grandma Marsha, and Uncle Norman. *I remember you. I love you.* Aunt Kathryn, you were my first writing teacher. You inspire me every day. Thank you for the gift of stories. And to my aunts and uncles and all my cousins, thank you for creating a world of magic and connection while we grew up, those stories are deep wells of inspiration. Thank you to Karla, for introducing me to a world of magic.

Jules Hinske, thank you for Avalon and for being a co-creator of that original childhood imagination landscape.

To the women and friendships in my life (named and unnamed), Hayley, Chrissy, Hannah, Sarah, Jackie, Emma, Adrienne, Sam, Heather, Lauren, Morgan, Olivia, Abby, Cydney, friends, sisters, cousins, chosen family. New York Coven: Ilana, Ashley, Michelle, Malu, Rachael, your spells, blessings and words of encouragement are everything.

To all the Witches of the Witch Wide Web (named and unnamed), I am so grateful to be connected to you and to learn from you.

To all my teachers (named and unnamed), thank you for your assigned readings, insights, prompts, guidance, support, critique, questions, and listening. *Thank you.* To sit in your classrooms was and is always an honor.

Especially to Laura Brownell, the high school guide I was lucky to have. Diane Seuss, you showed me the duende; Traci Brimhall for your poetic wisdom; Dr. Charlene Boyer-Lewis, you taught me the importance of history; Aracelis Girmay, you guided me to construct the altar; Suzanne Gardinier, your ferocity of being; Jeffrey McDaniel, your wise and patient ways; R. A. Villanueva, for your catalytic thinking; Matthea Harvey for your imagination; and Paige Ackerson-Kiely, your humor, insights, and wisdom have been a gift on my studying path.

Thank you to Rebecca Gordon and her incredible Astrology School, where I studied. Thank you to Liza Fenster for your education in energy healing. Thank you to Juliet Blankespoor and the team at Chestnut School of Herbal Medicine. Thank you to Kathryn Solie and her guidance on the poisonous plant path, and the study of plant magic paired with ritual.

Thank you to all my teachers outside the classroom. Delisha Upshaw, you are incredible. Thank you to the wonderful Ken Jordan (now passed through the veil), who invited me to New York City and helped me onto my path. Stephanie Wang, your guidance changed my life. Bobby Klein, I miss you all the time. Thanks for your blessings and for seeing this Witch. John Reed, for asking me "if I was bored" and introducing me to Ken and the magical world of New York City. Thank you, Veronica, fellow Word Witch.

I want to thank my friends at the Poetry Society of New York for giving me a poetry family in New York City. Xenia Viray, thank you for knowing this book before I did, for all our talks in the park that inspired so many of the threads woven here, and for your blessings of biophilia magic.

To all the Witches at Tamed Wild, but especially my dear friend Shelby Bundy, it is such a gift to create with you. To my fellow Word Witch and constant friend and collaborator,

Kristin Lisenby, you inspire me daily. Caitlyn Barone, coven sister, thank you.

I want to acknowledge your fierce and kind genius, Robin Rose Bennett, an incredible writer, Witch, mentor, and friend I have been so lucky to study with and know. This book is because of you. Your knowledge and guidance are great gifts on this Witch path, and to write with you, as sisters, is a blessing. I remember sitting in a circle at your house in March of 2021 and knowing I was taking a step toward something, but I was not sure what that was yet. Thank you to all the Witches and magic makers who sat in that circle. You all inspire me greatly. And my pomegranates, Nicla DiCosmo and Kate Sheldrick, Witch sisters.

Thank you Kara Rota and the team at Thompson Literary Agency. Kara, I could not have done this without your support, Word Witchery, and generous wisdom.

Thank you to the team at Hachette and Grand Central Publishing, and all of the editors, designers, and teamwork that made this book possible. Thank you, Gwen Hawkes, who saw the altar in the pages, and Carrie Napolitano and Natalie Bautista for your brilliant editorial eye, thank you, thank you.

To the writers of Salon Prosa, thank you for your supportive editorial eyes and encouragement through the journey.

Finally, thank you to my ancestors. Because you lived, met, loved, and died, I am alive to write this book. I think of you often and with gratitude. This is all because of and for you.

APPENDIX A

The Four Steps to Creating a Writing Ritual

Throughout this book, we have ritualized different aspects of our writing practice. If you're in need of some additional guidance in constructing your own writing ritual, you can use the below format to help you get started.

Step #1: ·•☽ Look to the Sky, Observe the Season ☾•·

The first place I start my writing ritual is with an observation of the stars and the season. I believe that Witches and magic makers, seers, and seekers live their lives by these cycles, and these happenings can help inform the timing of our rituals. For example, when there are eclipses, your rituals may be different from when there is a solstice or equinox, a full moon, or a new moon. Through tracking the seasonal shifts, you're naturally more connected to the earth (the earth is you) and, therefore, yourself. From this place, your natural knowing and intuition can speak more clearly through your language and words.

Step #2:
Set Your Intention

Setting an intention is a powerful way to infuse your writing ritual. An intention is often a clear, one-sentence statement that speaks aloud to the universe what you intend to practice in your ritual. Intentions are often best when they are concise and clear, and also embody the energy that you desire to cultivate in your practice. A good intention allows for the possibility beyond the sister of goal setting. It allows for the mystery to do its work.

Step #3:
Create Your Ritual Space

Once you are aware and connected to the energy at play, and you've set your intention for your writing ritual, create your ritual space. This can be writing with your back against a tree or your feet in the grass. It can be at the foot of an altar you've created for your writing practice, or it can be by candlelight to commune with your ancestors or your creative spirit and muse. Your ritual space can help you write and be present as you perform your ritual.

Step #4:
Write

Once your space is ready, you're ready to write. And write you must. A writing ritual can help you support your creativity, a channeling or divination practice through something like automatic writing, or help you hit a deadline for your novel or book. A ritual has the power to support these parts of ourselves that yearn to speak and can allow our creativity to flow. When you're done writing, allowing your pen to be guided by your ritual, intention, the stars, and the seasons, you can read what you've written or fold it up and put it on your altar until the next full moon. Writing by hand is always a beautiful way to engage your entire body in the process, but by computer or voice note is always a powerful and potent way to create, too.

APPENDIX B

Astrological Season Writing Prompts

This book was created as a companion for reigniting or building your magical and writing practice together. But I didn't want to send you out into the world without a year of seasonal rituals that you could write into and with.

Feel free to return to this part of the book whenever you need a spell, or a spark.

Below you'll find a prompt and example for each season and its corresponding elements and their modalities. Cardinal signs begin a season; they are often initiators. Fixed signs are steadfast and preserve, and happen in the middle of the season. Mutable signs occur at the end of a season, and they release and transform. The cardinal signs are Aries, Cancer, Libra, and Capricorn. The fixed signs are Taurus, Leo, Scorpio, and Aquarius. The mutable signs are Gemini, Virgo, Sagittarius, and Pisces. The fire signs are Aries, Leo, and Sagittarius. The earth signs are Taurus, Virgo, and Capricorn. The air signs are Gemini, Libra, and Aquarius. The water signs are Cancer, Scorpio, and Pisces.

•☽ Aries Season Writing Prompt ☾•

Aries season begins with the spring equinox between March 20 and March 23 each year. This change of seasons invites us to leave behind the dark moon and dreaming ocean of Pisces season. After completing this cycle, winter begins to thaw, and the wheel keeps turning. Aries is a cardinal fire sign (meaning a sign that ushers in a new season at solstice or equinox). Aries is the first sign of the zodiac, the astrological new year. The planetary ruler of Aries is Mars. Change is afoot. Magic is present, and a strike of the match and the lighting of a sacred fire says, *"Let's begin again."*

The etymology of spring as a noun came from the Middle English spryng meaning a wellspring, tide, branch, sunrise, snare, or a flock. I like to think of its origin, as the sacred water of the season that tends to the seeds, the spring rains, the new beginning rushing forth. For me, this is the true new year.

An invitation, Word Witch: *This spring, may you stir the soup of your origin stories giving way to new gods. May you bathe under the moon's light, an ancient rite, like a rabbit, a sacred sign of spring. May you call yourself a spring, both a spring of life-giving waters and a spring of poetic blossoms, bursting from the seeds you have sown. May all your intentions unfurl with divine knowing.*

A Writing Prompt for Aries Season

The Title: "The Start ____________"

Line 1: "Who ______________________________"
Line 2: "Earth ____________________________"
Line 3: "Kneeling __________________________"
Line 4: "Bonfire ___________________________"
Line 5: "I knew a way ______________________"
Line 6: "You can ___________________________"
Line 7: "Here a whisper ____________________"

The Start of a Cycle, We Begin Again

Who will meet me at the forest's edge?
Earth itself keeps asking me to listen
to the secrets. Kneeling here in the dirt,
I make a bonfire of my wishes.
I knew a way once to start a fire with laughter.
You can make a map with memories
penned by your intuition. Here, a whisper says,
"Spring, a song you once knew, asks
you to remember, sing along."

•☽ Taurus Season Writing Prompt ☾•

Taurus season begins each year between April 19 and April 23. If Aries season is the beginning of the astrological year, and the season of fresh starts when the seeds are planted, then Taurus season is when the roots take hold. This season encourages stillness, patience, and connection to slowness's divine power. Taurus is a fixed earth sign, meaning, Taurus season happens in the middle of the spring season, when the days become longer, much like the roots do. During this time, into the earth we go, as we simultaneously grow toward the warming sun. The planetary ruler of Taurus is Venus.

Taurus season's message is one of slowing down and living deliciously (wherever and however possible). Taurus asks us to revel in slowness in the garden under a darkening sky, to delight in each other, to hold the earth and be held in return. Taurus says, "There is no hurry. Death comes for us all. Pay attention, embrace opinion, and revel in delight." *It is divine to desire.* It is magical to be here, together.

This season encourages us to connect with our roots, to dig deep into ourselves and our bodies, and discover where we feel most creative and abundant, or where in our gardens we might need a little bit more love, nourishment, weeding, or shade.

An invitation, Word Witch: *Lounge about in the garden. Remember that luxury is slowness, and to take your time is divine. Plant flowers, plant poems, create a world dedicated to harmonious creativity. Listen, delight in your stubbornness. Allow yourself to unfurl like the season.*

A Writing Prompt for Taurus Season

The Title: "The Season of __________"

Line 1: "Slowness ______________________________"
Line 2: "Bare ______________________________"
Line 3: "The hands ______________________________"
Line 4: "Reaching ______________________________"
Line 5: "The story of ______________________________"
Line 6: "Possibility ______________________________"
Line 7: "Hello ______________________________"

The Season of Slowness, I Reach My Hands Up

Slowness is a spell. Barefooted I lope through
the grass in my mind. The hands of my body
holding hope, like the branches of a tree, reaching.
The story of my life unfolds. I unfold with it.
Possibility is a spell. Hello, dear earth, I give
over to the pleasure of our togetherness.

·•☽ Gemini Season Writing Prompt ☾•·

Gemini season begins between May 19 and May 23. Gemini is a mutable air sign. A mutable sign concludes a season, in this case, spring. To be mutable is to know how to celebrate endings. Gemini is swift in intellect, knows how to remain flexible, and can consistently move, change, and adapt with grace, curiosity, and a natural and inherent wisdom.

Gemini is the archetypal twin, representing the duality inside us, our shadow side, and the different ways we can show up in the world. When stars are born, they are always born as twins, as binary stars. Gemini is deeply connected to its planetary ruler, Mercury. There is both the astrological and the mythical Mercury. Both are messengers, carry information, and have a trickster element. The word "mercurial" means something unpredictable.

This month is a potent time to examine how your language mends, breaks, weaves, and travels. Mythical Mercury is known for transcending the binary on his winged sandals. Mercury's strangeness is a superpower.

An invitation, Word Witch: *Honor your curiosity. Ask questions, listen to the answers, and remember to embrace the power to change your mind. Take out your pen, tell your story, and seek new ways to communicate. Change is the only constant. Celebrate your wings.*

APPENDIX B

A Writing Prompt for Gemini Season

The Title: "I Take My ___________"

Line 1: "Listen, winds ___________________________"
Line 2: "Curiosity ______________________________"
Line 3: "Binary stars ___________________________"
Line 4: "Crossing _______________________________"
Line 5: "This stitch ____________________________"
Line 6: "When I listen __________________________"
Line 7: "Never _________________________________"

I Take My Pen and I Put It to Paper

Listen, winds, my imagination is awake
now. Curiosity which begins much like the
sun rises, over a horizon. Binary stars
when born, might think they are the other
(and we are). Cross the sky, a whipstitch,
the constellations bind us through stories.
When I listen to the leaves rustling, I know
I am never alone.

Cancer Season Writing Prompt

Cancer season begins each year between June 19 and June 23 and with it, the beginning of summer in the northern hemisphere.

Cancer is a cardinal (at the beginning of a season) water sign. This sign is known for its emotional depths, divine ties to the moon and lunar correspondences, and its archetypal vision for care and nourishment for the collective, which is why Cancerian energy is often given the label "the mother." The planetary ruler of Cancer is the moon.

Cancer is the crab, the shelled crustacean that moves between land and ocean, traversing the liminal place in between, intuitively understanding the tides, and stepping lightly betwixt and between.

The word "solstice" comes from the etymology of the "still sun." The sun stands still, the night is at its shortest, and dusk and dawn stretch, much like the magic of those solar rays.

An invitation, Word Witch: *I invite you to gather your plants, dance under the moon, howl, go feral, embrace all that is divine. This is a season to go barefoot, connect with the buzz of the natural world, go camping, build earth altars, and feel supported by that burgeoning sun.*

APPENDIX B

A Writing Prompt for Cancer Season

The Title: "Still ____________"

Line 1: "There is ______________________________"
Line 2: "Betwixt and ________________________"
Line 3: "Stones ______________________________"
Line 4: "Drawing ____________________________"
Line 5: "Sun ________________________________"
Line 6: "A Spell ____________________________"
Line 7: "Feral _______________________________"

Still, the Sun Rises

There is a dance in the solstice
betwixt and between, a crossroads
of seasons, standing stones frame
the shadows, drawing down the moon
to meet the sun. A spell of the summer
feral, I howl with my whole heart.

·•☽ Leo Season Writing Prompt ☾•·

Leo season begins each year between July 19 and July 23. Starting with a roar, Leo is associated with the archetypal lion and the sacred flame. It asks us to walk across the savannah of summer in the northern hemisphere, drink from the cup we call life, and create consciously and with all the wildness in our bones.

Leo is a fixed fire sign, which means that it corresponds with the element of fire and occurs between the solstice and equinox in the middle of a season.

Ruled by the Sun, Leo asks us to shine and to make. Leo is the energy of center stage, solar magic. Leo is truly the lion, the archetypal hunter, the member of the pack and pride, the soft-footed, wild-maned, the royalty of the more than human kingdom, our kin.

An invitation, Word Witch: *Seek that which inspires these next few weeks, find what is feral in your heart, and allow yourself to partner with the fire in sacred collaboration. Tend to the flame, look up at the sun, and feel yourself in love with summer and in love with your creativity.*

A Writing Prompt for Leo Season

The Title: "Sun Is ________"

Line 1: "Light ________________"
Line 2: "Inner wild ________________"
Line 3: "Lion ________________"
Line 4: "To roar ________________"
Line 5: "Skies ________________"
Line 6: "Whoever ________________"
Line 7: "Yearn ________________"

Sun Speaks

Light, which has its fingers, inner wild with its
untamed mane. All that is feral is the kingdom
of lions. To roar is to claim yourself.
Skies that bring the heat, the gift of life, here.
Whoever you are, find ways to make and to create.
With hands, the clay of the warm earth.
Yearn for the fire that licks at your rib cage,
that reminds you that you are alive.

·•☽ Virgo Season Writing Prompt ☾•·

Virgo season begins each year between August 19 and August 23 and is a mutable earth sign, occurring at the end of summer in the northern hemisphere. The planetary ruler of Virgo is Mercury.

Virgo is all about precision, but also about perception. Virgo loves to learn, pay attention, and investigate the details. This season happens during the harvest season, symbolized by the goddess holding a sheaf of wheat. A reminder that what we sow, we harvest.

An invitation, Word Witch: *Celebrate the endings of things, and find joy in the details. Peer into the portal with precision, trust that you know what to do, and know that magic can be found anywhere you go.*

A Writing Prompt for Virgo Season

The Title: "Letting Go ____________"

Line 1: "In each ______________________________"
Line 2: "Already ____________________________"
Line 3: "The air _____________________________"
Line 4: "Yesterday I _________________________"
Line 5: "And yes, tomorrow ___________________"
Line 6: "This too ____________________________"
Line 7: "Moments ____________________________"

Letting Go My Hands Not Tightly Grasping

In each season, a lesson already,
I breathe relief through nostrils
because the air changes, yes. Yesterday,
I dove into the water
and yes tomorrow, barefoot, resurface footing rock,
and this too is a lesson. Each moment a
making of this day.

Libra Season Writing Prompt

Libra season begins each year between September 19 and September 23, marking the autumn equinox in the northern hemisphere. Libra is a cardinal air season, meaning it occurs at the beginning of the fall season. Libra is ruled by the planet Venus.

The sign of Libra is symbolized by the only inanimate object in the zodiac, the divine scales of justice. Libra teaches that balance is not always about being balanced, but rather the way that the scales hang in the balance, shifting weight, adapting, and seeking harmony. Libra explores a measured approach. What some people might interpret as indecision from Libra placements is instead a deep honoring of all the decisions presented.

An invitation, Word Witch: *Seek out the milk and honey in life. What does harmony mean within your words? Discover the active practice of being in balance and bringing beauty wherever you go in the golden light of autumn.*

A Writing Prompt for Libra Season

The Title: "A Descent Into __________"

Line 1: "The beginning ______________________"
Line 2: "A moon ______________________"
Line 3: "I am not ______________________"
Line 4: "But instead ______________________"
Line 5: "That deep forest ______________________"
Line 6: "Look ______________________"
Line 7: "We leave ______________________"

A Descent into My Memories, a Different Kind of Underworld

The beginning of a season, I sense the light change,
a moon caught in the branches of an oak, a
kind of night-light.
I am not as young as I once was, but instead I
carry her with me.
We travel through that deep forest, the one
of my younger years.
Look, we pass by these trees as many times as we must.
We leave an offering of thank you at the
gnarled roots, still growing,
time passing, into another sacred autumn.

Scorpio Season Writing Prompt

Scorpio season begins each year between October 19 and October 23. Scorpio is a fixed water sign and occurs in the middle of a season, in fall. In traditional astrology, Scorpio is ruled by the planet Mars, and in modern astrology, Pluto.

Scorpio season loves a mystery. Scorpios live up to the saying that still waters run deep. Scorpio season encourages you to feel intensity and to know, in your bones, that depth, darkness, and underworld initiation are a gift. Symbolized by the scorpion, this sign dances with its intensity, and also its intuition.

An invitation, Word Witch: *This Scorpio season, dive deep. Connect ritually with water, celebrate your intensity, and let the waters guide your pen, leading you more deeply into your innate creative and intuitive nature.*

APPENDIX B

A Writing Prompt for Scorpio Season

The Title: "Water That ________"

Line 1: "Cycles of ______________________"
Line 2: "Life giving ____________________"
Line 3: "Water is ______________________"
Line 4: "There is no ____________________"
Line 5: "Tears ________________________"
Line 6: "Or even _______________________"
Line 7: "Blue _________________________"

Water That Pools in My Heart

Cycles of life, life-giving tides of our planet,
water is a teacher. There is no world
without water, tears, the language of our love
and grief. There is no joy without water,
or even, the sound proceeding it. The dull
roar of being human. I look at the
sky, blue as it stretches, reminding me of an
ocean, dancing above my head.

·•☽ Sagittarius Season Writing Prompt ☾•·

Sagittarius season begins each year between October 19 and October 23. Sagittarius is the symbolic archer, the metaphor of the bow and arrow. Sagittarius is a mutable sign (a sign at the end of a season), is ruled by the planet Jupiter, and is a fire sign.

Sagittarius is the archetypal centaur, half horse, half human, carrying a bow and arrow, the thudding of horse hooves across time and myth. It's no surprise that Sagittarius is linked with Jupiter, a planet that symbolizes wisdom, growth, and expansion. And much like their planetary ruler, the Sagittarius person is always looking for an adventure. Sagittarius seeks wisdom and yearns to experience the world.

An invitation, Word Witch: *The world invites you to learn, to listen, to explore and share. It's time for an adventure, whether of your feet or your heart. Follow what tugs at the soul strings.*

A Writing Prompt for Sagittarius Season

The Title: "A Bow and Arrow ____________"

Line 1: "Take aim ________________________________"
Line 2: "There is a flame ________________________"
Line 3: "Running ____________________________"
Line 4: "Remembering _________________________"
Line 5: "What burns __________________________"
Line 6: "Transformation _______________________"
Line 7: "Let's go, here _______________________"

A Bow and Arrow, I Seek a Dream

Take aim, strange one, there is a flame that never
goes out. Running into the dark of the room, embers.
Remembering all the past, the ashes, what
burns in the shadows
is a kind of transformation. The season is changing, again.
Let's go, here, I'll show you how to strike the match.

•☽ Capricorn Season Writing Prompt ☾•

Capricorn season begins between December 19 and December 23. Capricorn is a cardinal earth sign. Cardinal signs mark the beginning of a season and are seen as initiators, and this sign begins winter. Capricorn deeply understands and embraces the start of things. Capricorn is ruled by the planet Saturn. The mythical sea goat symbolizes Capricorn. Pictured with the body of a goat and with the tail of a fish, this being reminds you that you can be more than one thing—simultaneously.

Here in the northern hemisphere, the sky darkens early in the afternoon, sometimes feeling all-encompassing; however, you can connect with your inner light during this time. Capricorn season is a time to reaffirm that you believe in magic.

An invitation, Word Witch: *The earth supports your dreams. Take the steps guided by your magic. Return to your creation myth. Celebrate the dark and the shadows and the potency that exists there.*

A Writing Prompt for Capricorn Season

The Title: "Threshold of __________"

Line 1: "Winter is ____________________________"
Line 2: "A bird ____________________________"
Line 3: "A candle ____________________________"
Line 4: "Dancing ____________________________"
Line 5: "Wherever ____________________________"
Line 6: "I offer ____________________________"
Line 7: "My ____________________________"

Threshold of Winter, on the Altar I Offer This Poem

Winter is the dream space, is a song from
the throat, the wing
of a bird, the feather quiet after a snow.
Winter is a candle, wax pooling, the soft light,
a poem, a dancing shadow. Dance with me,
we are one. Wherever I go, the seasons of my life unfurl
like a palm. I offer this poem to that altar,
my love, my hands, these words, Winter
work your magic, yet again, I turn.

Aquarius Seasonal Writing Ritual

Aquarius season begins each year between January 19 and January 23. Aquarius is a fixed air sign. Fixed meaning that it comes in the middle of a season, in the midst of winter in the northern hemisphere. A fixed sign knows steadiness. Aquarius is the archetypal water bearer. Aquarius is the innovator, the rebel, the one who cares about the collective. In traditional astrology, Aquarius is ruled by Saturn, and in modern astrology, Uranus.

Aquarius celebrates that we are all individuals. But in our uniqueness and individuality, we are all the same. This sign celebrates the individual as a part of the larger collective. Aquarius knows we need each of us in our authentic magic to work together. Aquarius is a symbol of stepping into your strangeness. Aquarius knows that the way forward is weird, and the path ahead is paved with prayer. Aquarius teaches us, "You must fight for your dreams, and you must fight for your neighbor's dreams."

An invitation, Word Witch: *Sing your rebel yell, dance the dance only you know, and invite others along; creativity is born from being wyrd, and being wyrd means being knowing.*

A Writing Prompt for Aquarius Season

The Title: "Wind ________"

Line 1: "From this ______________________"
Line 2: "Following ______________________"
Line 3: "Vision ______________________"
Line 4: "Strangeness ______________________"
Line 5: "The collective ______________________"
Line 6: "Winds of ______________________"
Line 7: "Rebel ______________________"

Winds of Change That Blow Back

From this winter, my heart underground
is a seed. Following the root systems, I close
my eyes and trust my vision. Strangeness
is the fertile soil, the collective the humming
earth, the winds of change are here. They
wake up the rebel, that sleeps beneath
the surface, there with my beating heart.

·•☽ Pisces Seasonal Writing Ritual ☾•·

Pisces season arrives between February 19 and February 23. Pisces is the sign of the fish and also the poet. This ancient and crone-like sign appears with messages from the depths of things. Spring is almost here, *but not yet*. Winter usually has something to say before it departs, allowing the earth to soften again and the seeds to push above the dirt, silt, and soil.

Pisces is a mutable water sign. It arrives at the end of a season, just before the season changes. Pisces understands how to move between the worlds through a thinning veil, which is the last sign of the astrological year before Aries ushers a new year in. A mutable sign understands the power of release, letting go, and being intimately aware of the emotions and emotional state of others. Pisces has the power of intuition, and its energetic presence encourages you to listen to your intuitive voice, to dream, and to conjure. This sign embraces the magic of dreams in their full expressions. In traditional astrology, the planetary ruler of Pisces is Jupiter, and in modern astrology, it is Neptune. Pisces loves a mermaid, someone who isn't afraid to traverse the depths and shadows of things.

An invitation, Word Witch: *Commit to your wild and let go of what is ready to be offered to the rushing waters. Remember, you are of this galaxy, ancient and strange. Your dreams are guides and teachers; follow your intuition.*

APPENDIX B

A Writing Prompt for Pisces Season

The Title: "Dreamer ___________"

Line 1: "Depths of ___________________________"
Line 2: "Water, which _______________________"
Line 3: "Diving ____________________________"
Line 4: "No fear of _________________________"
Line 5: "Dreams ____________________________"
Line 6: "Messages __________________________"
Line 7: "Here ______________________________"

Dreamer, the Water Is Waiting

Depths of the time, water,
which is a great teacher. Diving
into the tides, I have no fear
of what waits there. My dreams
remind me, messages
from the beyond to listen, listen. Here
the cycles of everything, shown
in a single drop.

APPENDIX C

Full Moon Poetry Prompts

The full moon always happens in the opposite sign of the season, when the sun and moon oppose each other in the sky. For example, in Leo season, the full moon will be in Aquarius. In Libra season, the full moon will be in Aries. For every zodiac full moon placement, I've included lines that can help you build the scaffolding, or the vessel, for a seven-line poem, prayer, or blessing. Not all seasons of the year will match the seasons where you live, so feel empowered to shift the cyclicality of these pieces and to bend and break the rules. These prompts are here to inspire your writing; even as I make them and follow them, I find my way paving new paths. These are jumping-off points. Listen to the full moon, and see where your pen is guided. *There is no one right way to do this.*

·•☽ Aries Full Moon ☾•·

The Title: "The Moon and Fire ____________"

Line 1: "Creative __________________________"
Line 2: "Flame of _________________________"
Line 3: "Full _____________________________"
Line 4: "Candles that ______________________"
Line 5: "Whispers _________________________"
Line 6: "Begin ____________________________"
Line 7: "Moon ____________________________"

The Moon and Fire Both Know Change

Creative spark, flame of my own
fullness, is a fire moon. Candles
that sing a song of the sky,
whispers from the heaven take note.
Beginning again is a spell, the moon
blesses this ritual, alchemy of self.

•☽ Taurus Full Moon ☾•

The Title: "Earth That ____________"

Line 1: "Gardens of ______________________________"
Line 2: "Steadfast ______________________________"
Line 3: "Wherever ______________________________"
Line 4: "Spiraling ______________________________"
Line 5: "Moon ______________________________"
Line 6: "Barefooted, I ______________________________"
Line 7: "This cycle ______________________________"

Earth That Listens to the Moon

Gardens of my hope. I plant a seed,
a spell, for my own steadfast heart.
Wherever I walk, there is wild.
Spiraling paths lined by artemisia,
the moon weed. Barefooted, I feel
my fullness. This cycle,
I step through the wet grass.

·•☽ Gemini Full Moon ☾•·

The Title: "On Wings __________"

Line 1: "I travel ______________________________"
Line 2: "Air ________________________________"
Line 3: "From the east ________________________"
Line 4: "Weaving ____________________________"
Line 5: "There are ___________________________"
Line 6: "I hold ______________________________"
Line 7: "Wholeness ___________________________"

On Wings I Travel to Horizons

I travel by putting one foot down and then another,
winged ankles, air that softly tugs at my clothes,
from the east, there is a beginning, a start, but first
I weave. This story, it is mine, yours, ours.
There are so many stories. I hold my hands up to feel
that wind. Wholeness taught by the moon, always
present, but rather a trick of the light.

•☽ Cancer Full Moon ☾•

The Title: "Waters of ________"

Line 1: "Look, I am ________________________"
Line 2: "Clawed, even ____________________"
Line 3: "Emotions _______________________"
Line 4: In this line speak about tides
Line 5: "Moon means ___________________"
Line 6: "So this __________________________"
Line 7: "And maybe ______________________"

Waters of Change

Look, I am wading.
Clawed, even, beginning
with my emotions and then,
governed celestially, a tide.
Moon means my body.
So this, the waters of—
And maybe here a lesson.

·•☽ Leo Full Moon ☾•·

The Title: "Full Moon ___________"

Line 1: "Lions ______________________________"
Line 2: "A candle in ________________________"
Line 3: "Do not fear _________________________"
Line 4: "This moon that ______________________"
Line 5: "A dance ____________________________"
Line 6: "Full _______________________________"
Line 7: "Fire _______________________________"

Full Moon of My Lion Heart

Lions know things. They are a candle
in the window, beckoning. A symbol
of this moon that teaches me to roar.
A dance of my wild, I shake my hair
out, fully myself, fire in my feet, as
I twirl into the night.

·•☽ Virgo Full Moon ☾•·

The Title: "Full Moon of __________"

Line 1: "Pay attention ______________________"
Line 2: "Listen ______________________"
Line 3: "Calling upon ______________________"
Line 4: "There was ______________________"
Line 5: "When I go ______________________"
Line 6: "Looking up ______________________"
Line 7: "Earth ______________________"

Full Moon of Tender Lessons

Pay attention, the sky has something
To tell you. Listen, it's been waiting,
a long time, calling your name. There was
a time, before, and there will be a time after.
When I go, I look up, and there,
from earth, I will go, there.

·•☽ Libra Full Moon ☾•·

The Title: "The Scales ____________"

Line 1: "Harmony ______________________________"
Line 2: "Like a rose ____________________________"
Line 3: "Wholeness ____________________________"
Line 4: "There are many _________________________"
Line 5: "Scales _______________________________"
Line 6: "Divine _______________________________"
Line 7: "Night, again ___________________________"

The Scales Dance in Balance

Harmony is an active practice. Like
a rose, it blooms into wholeness,
when the conditions are right. There
are many ways to be true. Scales
tip toward each other saying hello,
divine dance under this moon.
Night, again comes. Night, again goes.

•●☽ Scorpio Full Moon ☾●•

The Title: "Darkness, Which ____________"

Line 1: "The Underworld ________________________"
Line 2: "This poem ____________________________"
Line 3: "Welcoming ___________________________"
Line 4: "The feeling ___________________________"
Line 5: "Moon, that ___________________________"
Line 6: "Sweetness ____________________________"
Line 7: "Shadow ______________________________"

Darkness, Which Is Held in My Hands

The Underworld is singing. It sings this poem,
welcoming the darkness, before moonrise.
The feeling of dirt in the hands and to hear
the whispers of earthworms is a gift. Moon,
that arrives in the sky in fullness, sweetness
(which is sometimes strange).
"Shadow self. I have expected you.
Dance with me to this song."

Sagittarius Full Moon

The Title: "A Quiver ________"

Line 1: "Archer that ________"
Line 2: "Moon calling ________"
Line 3: "Burning ________"
Line 4: "Here ________"
Line 5: "Wherever I go ________"
Line 6: "Hearing ________"
Line 7: "Stillness ________"

A Quiver of Fire

Archer that I have always been. I wait
to hear that moon calling.
Burning the fire of all I no longer carry,
here, I knew the exactly right moment.
This and this and this . . . Wherever I go,
there I am. Hearing my own lungs expand—
then. Stillness, I am my own moon. The fire
casts a haunting (a deep breath) and teaching shadow.

·•☽ Capricorn Full Moon ☾•·

The Title: "Full Moon ____________"

Line 1: "I remember ____________________________"
Line 2: "A summer of _________________________"
Line 3: "When I put _________________________"
Line 4: "There is ______________________________"
Line 5: "Heat _________________________________"
Line 6: "I walk _______________________________"
Line 7: "Moon ________________________________"

Full Moon, the Earth Is Humming

I remember the summers
of my past summers of scraped knees
and lush oak trees over
my sleeping bed. When
I put my ear to the earth,
the fireflies remind me
of that girl (still me). There
is much to remember. Heat
of summer is a spell. I walk through
that field of my memory.
Moon lights my way.

·•☽ Aquarius Full Moon ☾•·

The Title: "The Moon ___________"

Line 1: "Look to the ___________________________"
Line 2: "The winds of _________________________"
Line 3: "Magic ______________________________"
Line 4: "Ancient _____________________________"
Line 5: "There is _____________________________"
Line 6: "Wherever ____________________________"
Line 7: "Whole ______________________________"

The Moon Is Ancient, She Sings an Old Song

Look to the sky, sea. The winds of strange
like rippling currents. Magic is stars, is ancient
stories. There is no wrong way to be you.
Wherever you go there you are. Whole
eternities exist inside your heart, palm open.

Pisces Full Moon

The Title: "Departure ____________"

Line 1: "The path ________________________________"
Line 2: "Change ________________________________"
Line 3: "Speak ________________________________"
Line 4: "This dream ________________________________"
Line 5: "Shadows ________________________________"
Line 6: "The moon ________________________________"
Line 7: "Leaving ________________________________"

Departure, the Eclipses Are Lanterns

The path appears
underfoot, like moss.
Change is a match struck
for a candle on the altar.
Speak your dream into
existence; this dream
of this life. Shadows cast
across the kitchen floor
from that moon. The moon
who sighs, reminding me
of my phases. I am sliver,

I am full. I am cycles
leaving each day at
the door of my life
like an armful of sunflowers.

APPENDIX D

New Moon Poetry Prompts

The new moon always happens in the sign of the season, when the sun and moon meet up in the sky. This is the first day of the lunar cycle. The moon is new, the cycle begins again. For example, in Pisces season, the new moon will be a new moon in Pisces. In Gemini season, the new moon will be in Gemini. For every zodiac new moon placement, I've included lines that can help you build the scaffolding, or the vessel, for a seven-line poem, prayer, or blessing. Not all seasons of the year will match the seasons where you live, so feel empowered to shift the cyclicality of these pieces and to bend and break the rules. These prompts are here to inspire your writing; even as I make them and follow them, I find my way paving new paths. These are jumping-off points. Listen to the full moon, and see where your pen is guided. *There is no one right way to do this.*

•☽ Aries New Moon ☾•

The Title: "The Start ____________"

Line 1: "Who ______________________________"
Line 2: "Earth ______________________________"
Line 3: "Kneeling ___________________________"
Line 4: "Bonfire _____________________________"
Line 5: "I knew a way _______________________"
Line 6: "You can ____________________________"
Line 7: "Here, a whisper _____________________"

The Start of a Cycle, We Begin Again

Who will meet me at the forest's edge?
Earth itself keeps asking me to listen
to the secrets. Kneeling here in the dirt,
I make a bonfire of my wishes.
I knew a way once to start a fire with laughter.
You can make a map with memories
penned by your intuition. Here, a whisper says,
"Spring, a song you once knew, asks you to remember,
sing along."

·•☽ Taurus New Moon ☾•·

The Title: "Myth of ________"

Line 1: "In spring, I ______________________"
Line 2: "A way through ___________________"
Line 3: "The stars _______________________"
Line 4: "Beginning ______________________"
Line 5: "Horizon ________________________"
Line 6: "Creature _______________________"
Line 7: "Story __________________________"

Myth of My Life, I Put My Pen to Paper

In spring, I am writing a way through. I look
up to the stars to remember my beginning.
The page is a horizon, the constellations, speak.
Creature of the ink, maker of the worlds,
story that wants to sing, now sing.

·☽ Gemini New Moon ☾·

The Title: "The Beginning ____________"

Line 1: "Waves of ______________________________"
Line 2: "Moon that ______________________________"
Line 3: "Churning ______________________________"
Line 4: "A tide ______________________________"
Line 5: "Listen ______________________________"
Line 6: "There is ______________________________"
Line 7: "The center ______________________________"

The Beginning of a Wave Starts Somewhere

Waves of my own making,
moon that knows my name.
Churning waters that give birth
to new tidepools. Listen,
the water is trying to tell us something.
There is an endless drum,
which lives in the center of our bodies.

·•☽ Cancer New Moon ☾•·

The Title: "Deep ________"

Line 1: "Water of ________"
Line 2: "Beginnings ________"
Line 3: "I write ________"
Line 4: "A song ________"
Line 5: "Depth ________"
Line 6: "Never ________"
Line 7: "Holding ________"

Deep Waters of the Sky

Water of the stars, beginnings of a new
story. I write this one myself. A song
of myself. Depth is a way to keep going,
passing by each underworld gate. Never
a question of if but when. Holding my breath
for just a moment before diving.

·•☽ Leo New Moon ☾•·

The Title: "Darkness, ____________"

Line 1: "A cycle of ______________________________"
Line 2: "Old stories ______________________________"
Line 3: "My wild ______________________________"
Line 4: "Reclamation ______________________________"
Line 5: "Named ______________________________"
Line 6: "And until ______________________________"
Line 7: "Where ______________________________"

Darkness, Another Name for Magic (Mystery)

A cycle of the tides, these waters bring
me old stories. My dark moon phase,
my wild, a pack of wolves, a screeching owl
reclamation comes in many forms. I long
to name myself, free. And I kneel at the altar
until I bear that name. Wherever you find
me, the wolves follow close, the kind of shadow
that I have always wanted for myself.

•◐ Virgo New Moon ◑•

The Title: "The Earth Teaches __________"

Line 1: "The roots ______________________________"
Line 2: "Looking in a new ______________________"
Line 3: "Through the trees _____________________"
Line 4: "The moon goes dark ___________________"
Line 5: "Patience ______________________________"
Line 6: "The harvest ___________________________"
Line 7: "End of _______________________________"

The Earth Teaches Me How to Keep a Secret

The roots they whisper, here, this is
how you can look in a new way, through
the trees, there is a horizon, the moon goes
dark, there each month. Patience is a spell,
the kind that knows just when the harvest
is ready, how to end a season, how to keep a secret.

•☽ Libra New Moon ☾•

The Title: "Scales That Bring ____________"

Line 1: "Balance is ______________________________"
Line 2: "Harmony, ____________________________"
Line 3: "Begin ______________________________"
Line 4: "To bring ____________________________"
Line 5: "Both hands __________________________"
Line 6: "A kind of ___________________________"
Line 7: "Walk _______________________________"

Scales That Bring Changes Are Always in Balance

Balance is a blessing. Much like harmony,
the song that tugs at the heart to begin again.
To bring yourself to the altar of the moon
both hands empty, yet open is a kind of gift.
Walk with a ready heart. You are in balance,
when you are yourself.

•◗ Scorpio New Moon ◖•

The Title: "What Is Ancient ___________"

Line 1: "The rocks ______________________________"
Line 2: "Spaces between _________________________"
Line 3: "The moon begins ________________________"
Line 4: "The earth _____________________________"
Line 5: "I hold ________________________________"
Line 6: "Like a scorpion ________________________"
Line 7: "My body, dirt, ________________________"

What Is Ancient Has Always Loved the Moon

The rocks they reach, mountains churning against
a horizon. In the spaces between, a new moon rises.
The moon begins again, and so we can too. The earth
holds us in our beginnings. I hold the
earth in my hands.
The dirt is my ancestors, your ancestors, our ancestors.
Like a scorpion, I create, I begin,
resilient. My body, dirt,
the moon, I crane my neck up,
a reaching stone myself.

·•☽ Sagittarius New Moon ☾•·

The Title: "Imagination ____________"

Line 1: "The dream ________________________________"
Line 2: "Winter ________________________________"
Line 3: "Bonfire ________________________________"
Line 4: "A match ________________________________"
Line 5: "Underfoot ______________________________"
Line 6: "The cold ________________________________"
Line 7: "Imagination is ___________________________"

Imagination Is a Form of Wintering

The dream of the dream glitters like snow.
Winter is a lesson in the creative process.
Bonfire of my heart, a match is lit in the
darkest night. Underfoot, the ground makes the sound
when it is really, really cold. The cold holds me,
both young and ancient. Imagination is
a way to survive,
a form of wintering.

·•☽ Capricorn New Moon ☾•·

The Title: "Renewal ____________"

Line 1: "Between the branches ____________________"
Line 2: "A river of __________________________"
Line 3: "This dance __________________________"
Line 4: "Spirals ____________________________"
Line 5: "Change is __________________________"
Line 6: "The song ___________________________"
Line 7: "Renewal ___________________________"

Renewal Comes in Many Forms

Between the branches
of the trees, bare in winter,
under a new moon,
there is a river of stars and sky.
This dance of seasons pulls me
deep into the spiral (of all things).
This path, which calls
for rest right now reminds me that
even when we sleep, we dream.
Change is happening
under the earth, alchemy of the soil.
The song I sing to myself is an old
one. Renewal is snow, it is dirt,
it is winter. It hums beneath my feet.

••☽ Aquarius New Moon ☾••

The Title: "Winter Still ____________"

Line 1: "There is ______________________________"
Line 2: "Lean into this __________________________"
Line 3: "Across a threshold ______________________"
Line 4: "Looking ______________________________"
Line 5: "I remember ___________________________"
Line 6: "Beginnings ___________________________"
Line 7: "I wait _______________________________"

Winter Still Lingers Its Cold Against My Skin

There is winter still, who knocks at my
door with its stillness.
"Lean into this," the seasons whisper. And so
I do, into darkness
across a threshold, I step, with meaning.
Looking at my hands
I remember each pass across winter,
beginnings happen under
the soil before spring. Beginnings happen slowly.
I wait to begin again.

•☽ Pisces New Moon ☾•

The Title: "Where There Is ____________"

Line 1: "Water, which ________________________"
Line 2: "A dream begins ____________________"
Line 3: "In darkness ________________________"
Line 4: "Seeds, which ______________________"
Line 5: "Listen, ___________________________"
Line 6: "The tide __________________________"
Line 7: "Depth ____________________________"

Where There Is Water, There Must Be Tides

Water, which knows cycles.
A dream begins
almost always in darkness.
Seeds, which I plant
in the soil soon,
but not yet. I keep
in my pocket. Listen, the sea
is lapping again at the shore.
Listen, the tide is turning,
and soon, things will

change again. Depth
is a teacher. I kneel
at the altar of the end
of this season. I open
my hands, palms facing the sky.

APPENDIX E

A Ritual:
Calling Your Energy Back

One of my favorite rituals to practice when I'm feeling ungrounded in my practice as either a writer or a Witch or both is a "A Calling Your Energy Back Ritual." This ritual exists in as many different forms and iterations as there are practitioners, but this is my take on this practice.

This is a simple ritual that you can keep in your magical toolbox to rely on when you're feeling ungrounded, scattered, or as if parts of your energetic body have been left behind in external conversations, contracts, or agreements that you've made over time.

Sometimes, without realizing it, our energy can become fragmented, and this simple mantra, ritual, and invocation can be all that is needed to remind the individual of their sovereignty and wholeness.

First, become grounded in your space (however you best do that), take a deep breath (or a few), allow yourself to arrive in the present moment, turn off the distractions in your space (if you're able), and call on any guides, ancestors, or deities that you have a relationship with. If you're in a more chaotic environment, that's okay, too—just do the best you can with whatever you have.

•☽ The Calling Your Energy Back Invocation ☾•

Speak aloud…

I call all my energy back to myself
from all commitments, known and unknown
all past lives, known and unknown
all realms, known and unknown
and from all that surrounds me, no matter the intention.

I am a sovereign being. I honor myself,
my joy, and my existence here on earth.
I call all my energy back. I am whole,
full, and divine.

So mote it be or something better.

Repeat daily as needed, knowing that you are always whole, and that can never be taken away from you. And if you feel called to, write your own version of this invocation in your voice.

When these affirmations are done in the practitioner's words and imbued with specific intentions, they can even be more powerful than following an original script. Although it can feel intimidating to alter or craft your own spells, know that there are many ways to do so and that the most important part is sincerity.

NOTES

Chapter One: Word Witches

1. Risa Dickens and Amy Torok, *Missing Witches: Recovering True Histories of Feminist Magic* (North Atlantic Books, 2021).
2. Tom Robbins, *Even Cowgirls Get the Blues: A Novel* (Bantam, 2003).
3. Muriel Rukeyser, *The Speed of Darkness* (Vintage, 1968).
4. Risa Dickens and Amy Torok, *Missing Witches: Recovering True Histories of Feminist Magic* (North Atlantic Books, 2021).
5. Frances Denny, *Major Arcana: Portraits of Witches in America* (Andrews McMeel Publishing, 2020).
6. Pam Grossman, *Waking the Witch: Reflections on Women, Magic, and Power* (Gallery Books, 2020).
7. Stephen King, *On Writing* (Simon and Schuster, 2002).
8. Kristin Lisenby and Kate Belew, hosts. *Magick & Alchemy*, Tamed Wild.
9. Native-Land.ca, accessed March 18, 2025. https://native-land.ca/.
10. Starhawk, *The Spiral Dance: A Rebirth of the Ancient Religion of the Great Goddess* (HarperCollins Publishers, 1979).

Chapter Two: What Is an Altar?

1. Aracelis Girmay, MFA Poetry Workshop. Sarah Lawrence College, 2019.
2. Joanna Cole, *The Magic School Bus Inside the Human Body* (Scholastic, 1990).
3. "Theoi Greek Mythology: Artemis' Treasures," *Theoi Greek Mythology*, accessed March 18, 2025. https://www.theoi.com/Olympios/ArtemisTreasures.html.
4. Amanda Yates Garcia, *Mystery Cult*, Substack, accessed March 18, 2025. https://amandayatesgarcia.substack.com/.

Chapter Three: The Foundation

1. "Agios Ioannis Spiliotis Church," Greeka.com, accessed March 18, 2025. https://www.greeka.com/cyclades/antiparos/sightseeing/agios-ioannis-spiliotis-church/.

2. "Home," Ghost Ranch, accessed March 18, 2025. https://www.ghostranch.org/.
3. Sarah Greenough, ed., *My Faraway One: Selected Letters of Georgia O'Keeffe and Alfred Stieglitz* (Yale University Press, 2011).
4. "Ritual." Merriam-Webster.com Dictionary. Accessed May 13, 2025. https://www.merriam-webster.com/dictionary/ritual.
5. The Research Council of Norway, "World's Oldest Ritual Discovered -- Worshipped the Python 70,000 Years Ago," *ScienceDaily*, November 30, 2006. Accessed May 13, 2025. https://www.sciencedaily.com/releases/2006/11/061130081347.htm.
6. Catherine Beyer, "The 5 Elemental Symbols: Fire, Water, Air, Earth, and Spirit," Learn Religions. Last modified May 17, 2024. https://www.learnreligions.com/elemental-symbols-4122788.
7. Stephen Arroyo, *Astrology, Psychology, and the Four Elements: An Energy Approach to Astrology & Its Use in the Counseling Arts* (CRCS Publications: 1978).
8. Robin Rose Bennett, *Healing Magic: A Green Witch Guidebook* (Sterling Publishing, 2004).
9. Bradley Laura, "Joan Didion's Essential Packing List," *AnOther*, January 7, 2015. https://www.anothermag.com/fashion-beauty/4230/joan-didion-s-essential-packing-list.
10. Rainer Maria Rilke, *Letters to a Young Poet* (W. W. Norton & Company, 1993).

Chapter Four: Air

1. Richard Powers, *The Overstory* (Penguin Group, 2024).
2. Terry Tempest Williams, *Refuge: An Unnatural History of Family and Place* (Vintage, 1992).
3. Paul Celan, "The Meridian," translated by Pierre Joris, 1960. PDF. Accessed May 13, 2025. https://media.sas.upenn.edu/afilreis/Celan-Paul_The-Meridian_1960.pdf.
4. Edmund De Waal, *The White Road: A Pilgrimage of Sorts* (Chatto & Windus, 2015).
5. Kate Murphy and Cynthia Susalla, "Secrets of Ancient Magic," *Expedition Magazine* 58, no. 1 (May 2016), accessed May 7, 2025. https://www.penn.museum/sites/expedition/secrets-of-ancient-magic/.

Chapter Five: Fire

1. Brian Handwerk, "Ice Age Artists May Have Used Firelight to Animate

Carvings," *Smithsonian*, April 20, 2022. https://www.smithsonianmag.com/science-nature/ice-age-artists-may-have-used-firelight-to-animate-carvings-180979943/.

2. Luba Mullen, "How Trees Survive and Thrive After a Fire," National Forest Foundation, accessed March 18, 2025. https://www.nationalforests.org/our-forests/light-and-seed-magazine/how-trees-survive-and-thrive-after-a-fire.
3. "History," National Candle Association, accessed March 18, 2025. https://candles.org/history/.
4. Alexander Afanasyev, *Vasilisa the Beautiful and Baba Yaga (Illustrated by Ivan Bilibin)* (The Planet, 2011).
5. Clarissa Pinkola Estés, PhD, *Women Who Run with the Wolves: Myths and Stories of the Wild Woman Archetype* (Ballantine Books, 1996).
6. Starhawk, *The Spiral Dance: A Rebirth of the Ancient Religion of the Great Goddess* (HarperCollins Publishers, 1979).
7. Kristin Lisenby, "Kristin Lisenby," https://www.kristinlisenby.com/.
8. Clarissa Pinkola Estés, "We Were Made for These Times," Awakin.org, accessed March 18, 2025. https://www.awakin.org/v2/read/view.php?tid=2195.
9. "Fuji (Planchette Writing)," EPFL Graph Search, accessed March 18, 2025. https://graphsearch.epfl.ch/en/concept/15499159.
10. "Automatic Writing," *Encyclopaedia Britannica*. Last modified March 18, 2025. https://www.britannica.com/topic/automatic-writing.
11. "Surrealism," *Encyclopaedia Britannica*. Last modified February 10, 2025. https://www.britannica.com/art/Surrealism.
12. "André Breton, Father of Surrealism." Surrealism Art, accessed March 18, 2025. https://www.surrealismart.org/history/andre-breton.html.
13. "André Breton," Poetry Foundation. Last modified November 13, 2020. https://www.poetryfoundation.org/poets/andre-breton.
14. André Breton, *Manifestoes of Surrealism* (University of Michigan Press, 1969).
15. Alex Pappademas, "This Must Be David Byrne," *GQ*, April 16, 2018. https://www.gq.com/story/david-byrne-talking-heads-icon-profile.
16. Ryan H. Walsh, "Read an Excerpt from Ryan H. Walsh's New Book on Van Morrison's *Astral Weeks*." *Stereogum*, March 18, 2025. https://www.stereogum.com/1986940/read-an-excerpt-from-ryan-h-walshs-new-book-on-van-morrisons-astral-weeks/columns/sounding-board/book-club/.
17. Marina Magloire, "The Spirit Writing of Lucille Clifton." *The Paris Review*,

October 19, 2020. https://www.theparisreview.org/blog/2020/10/19/the-spirit-writing-of-lucille-clifton/.

18. Erin Glogowski, "Spirit Writing, Body Problems: Lucille Clifton's Faith," *Rose Library News*, July 13, 2022. https://scholarblogs.emory.edu/marbl/2022/07/13/spirit-writing-body-problems-lucille-cliftons-faith/.

Chapter Six: Water

1. Heidi Smith, *The Uncommon Book of Prayer: A Guide to Co-Creating with the Universe* (Hachette UK, 2024).
2. "Ocean Worlds," NASA, https://www.nasa.gov/specials/ocean-worlds/.
3. Myths of Creation, accessed March 18, 2025. https://mythsofcreation.com/.
4. Sarah Faith Gottesdiener, *The Moon Book: Lunar Magic to Change Your Life* (Macmillan + ORM, 2020).
5. Demetra George, *Mysteries of the Dark Moon: The Healing Power of the Dark Goddess* (HarperOne, 1992).

Chapter Seven: Earth

1. Robin Rose Bennett, *The Gift of Healing Herbs* (North Atlantic Books, 2014).
2. Asia Suler, *Mirrors in the Earth: Reflections on Self-Healing from the Living World* (North Atlantic Books, 2022).
3. Felicia Cocotzin Ruiz, *Earth Medicines: Ancestral Wisdom, Healing Recipes, and Wellness Rituals from a Curandera* (Shambhala Publications, 2021).
4. Robin Wall Kimmerer, *Braiding Sweetgrass: Indigenous Wisdom, Scientific Knowledge and the Teachings of Plants*, hardcover special ed. (Milkweed Editions, 2020).
5. Mary Oliver, *American Primitive* (Back Bay Books, 1983).
6. Ross Gay, *The Book of Delights: Essays on the Small Joys We Overlook in Our Busy Lives* (Hodder Paperbacks, 2020).
7. Mary Oliver, *Devotions* (Corsair, 2023).
8. Louise Glück, *The Wild Iris* (HarperCollins, 2022).
9. Conrad Hilberry, *The Fingernail of Luck: Poems* (Mayapple Press, 2005).
10. Bhanu Kapil, "Master Class," *Sarah Lawrence College*, 2019.
11. Victoria Redel, "Marie Howe: Interview," *BOMB Magazine*, October 1, 1997. https://bombmagazine.org/articles/1997/10/01/marie-howe/.
12. "Tips for Reading." Emily Dickinson Museum. https://www.emilydickinsonmuseum.org/emily-dickinson/poetry/tips-for-reading/.

13. Ralph Waldo Emerson, "The Poet," in *Essays and Lectures*, William H. Gilman (Library of America, 1983), 405–421.
14. Louise Bourgeois, *What Is the Shape of This Problem?* 1999. https://www.moma.org/collection/works/series/84398.
15. Aracelis Girmay, "Poetry Workshop," Sarah Lawrence College, 2018.
16. Gregory Orr and Ellen Bryant Voigt, *Poets Teaching Poets: Self and the World* (University of Michigan Press, 1996).
17. Annie Finch, *How to Scan a Poem: A Poetry Witch Workbook* (Poetry Witch Press, 2023).
18. Anne Waldman, *Fast Speaking Woman: Chants and Essays: Pocket Poets Number 33* (City Lights Books, 1996).
19. Gwendolyn Brooks, *The Bean Eaters* (Hassell Street Press, 1917, 2021).
20. Dana Levin (@danalevinpoet), "If you're a writer, you must write," Facebook, February 18, 2025, https://www.facebook.com/danalevinpoet/posts/pfbid029Cs2fuEhLf9u3CzkYiEKucAgzpJbvR7eQiktiphdyPa51hJCeaBaDZFQyhwwiqysl?rdid=j1HbbPumat7RPxCF#.

Chapter Eight: Spirit

1. Jessica Hundley and Pam Grossman, *Witchcraft. The Library of Esoterica* (Taschen, 2021).
2. *My So-Called Life*. Pilot episode. Directed by Winnie Holzman. Aired August 25, 1994. ABC.
3. "Enheduanna: The World's First Named Author." *BBC Culture*, October 25, 2022. https://www.bbc.com/culture/article/20221025-enheduanna-the-worlds-first-named-author.
4. Enheduanna and Betty De Shong Meador, *Inanna, Lady of Largest Heart: Poems of the Sumerian High Priestess Enheduanna* (University of Texas Press, 2000).
5. Enheduanna and Betty De Shong Meador, *Princess, Priestess, Poet: The Sumerian Temple Hymns of Enheduanna* (University of Texas Press, 2009).
6. John Keats, "This Living Hand, Now Warm and Capable," Poetry Foundation, accessed March 18, 2025. https://www.poetryfoundation.org/poems/50375/this-living-hand-now-warm-and-capable.
7. Sophie Strand, *The Flowering Wand: Rewilding the Sacred Masculine* (Simon and Schuster, 2022).
8. *Grief Spells Newsletter*, Substack, accessed March 18, 2025. https://griefspells.substack.com/.
9. Ethan Richardson, "Nick Cave on Why Most Love Songs Are Hate Songs,"

Mockingbird, January 29, 2014. https://mbird.com/music/nick-cave-on-why-most-love-songs-are-hate-songs/.

10. Federico García Lorca, *In Search of Duende* (New Directions Pearls, 2010).
11. Kate Belew and Kristin Lisenby, "Episode 116: The Veil Is Thin," *Magick & Alchemy*. October 18, 2023. https://podcasts.apple.com/us/podcast/episode-116-the-veil-is-thin/id1540643661?i=1000631719249.
12. Danielle Dulsky, *The Night House: Folklore, Fairy Tales, Rites, and Magick for the Wise and Wild* (New World Library, 2025).
13. Excerpted from *New Weathers: Poetics from the Naropa Archive*, edited by Anne Waldman and Emma Gomis (Nightboat Books, 2022).
14. Maia Toll, *The Night School: Lessons in Moonlight, Magic, and the Mysteries of Being Human* (Running Press Adult, 2022).
15. Stephen Langdon, "A Babylonian Dream Tablet on the Interpretation of Dreams." *The Museum Journal* 8, no. 2 (1917): 15–24. https://www.penn.museum/documents/publications/journal/08-2/babylonian_tablet_dreams.pdf.

INDEX

activism, 146–147
affirmations, 54, 55
air
about, 59–63
associations and, 44–45
calling a circle and, 43–44
introduction to, 42
ritual and, 64–65
spell crafting and, 67–70
on Word Witch altar, 63–64
in writing practice, 65–67
air signs, 197
All Souls' Day (Dia de los Muertos), 110
altars
about, 23–24
air and, 63–64
ancestors and, 157, 161–165
building, 21, 25–27
earth and, 116–118, 124
elegies and, 168–169
empty hands and, 171–173
fire and, 78–79
foundation and, 34–37, 39–40
intentions and, 31–32
making for writing practice, 28–30
offerings and, 165–166, 169–170
spirit and, 161–165
symbolic actions and correspondences and, 30–31
water and, 98–99, 170
what you bring to, 27–28
ancestors, 153–165, 178
anchor statements, 92
Aquarius, 45, 197, 218–219, 234, 248
Aries, 45, 106, 107, 197, 198–199, 224, 238
Arroyo, Stephen, 42–43
Artemis, 177
astrology, 44–46, 197–221. *See also individual signs*
Astrology, Psychology, and the Four Elements (Arroyo), 42–43
atemwende, 66
attention, offering, 120–123, 125–127
automatic writing, 88–93, 104–105, 162, 170
autumn equinox, 109

Baba Yaga, 80–85, 172
"Beginning of a Wave Starts Somewhere, The," 240
Belew, Kevin, 155
Beltane, 107
Bennett, Robin Rose, 9, 18, 47–48, 51, 118, 119
bibliomancy, 162–163

INDEX

birds, 61–63
Blake, William, 177
blessings
  of beginning, 39–40
  examples of, 72–73
  gratitude and, 71–72
  as a spell, 71–72
bones, 80, 172
Book of Delights, The (Gay), 123
books, 156, 162–163
Bourgeois, Louise, 135
"Bow and Arrow, I Seek a Dream, A," 215
Braiding Sweetgrass (Kimmerer), 120
breath, 59–61, 65–67. *See also* air
Breton, André, 90
Brigid, 111
Brooks, Gwendolyn, 145–146
Bundy, Shelby, 87
butterflies, 129
Byrne, David, 90

Cailleach, 177
calling a circle, 43, 47–51
Cancer, 46, 108, 197, 204–205, 227, 241
candles, 78–79
Capricorn, 46, 110, 197, 216–217, 233, 247
cardinal signs, 197
Carrington, Leonora, 90
Casa Azul, 38
Cave, Nick, 175
cedar, as gift of thanks, 119
Celan, Paul, 66
channeled writing. *See* automatic writing
Chase, Angela, 152
Church of Agios Ioannis Spiliotis (Saint John of the Cave), 35
circles
  calling, 43, 47–51
  opening, 187
Clifton, Lucille, 90–91, 161
Cohen, Leonard, 175
collecting phase, 15
community, 13
consumption culture, 119
cord-cutting release ritual, 53–54
correspondences, 30–31
creative ancestors, 156–162
creativity, 7, 75, 77, 84, 85, 98, 116, 173, 181
cross-quarter days, 105, 107, 108–110, 111
crossroads, 16
curiosity, 3
cycles
  calling upon, 100–101
  of moon, 96, 98, 101–105
  rain, 97–98
  seasonal, 105–112

Dalí, Salvador, 90
dark moon, 101, 105, 111–112
"Darkness, Another Name for Magic (Mystery)," 242
"Darkness, Which Is Held in My Hands," 231
"Deep Waters of the Sky," 241
delight, 123
Denny, Frances F., 12–13
"Departure, the Eclipses Are Lanterns," 235–236
"Descent into My Memories, a Different Kind of Underworld, A," 211

Dia de los Muertos (All Souls' Day), 110
Dickens, Risa, 10
Dickinson, Emily, 2, 132–133, 161, 170
Didion, Joan, 52
divination, author's first encounter with, 4
dolphins, 60
Dominguez, Ivo, Jr., 151
doubt, 171
"Dreamer, the Water Is Waiting," 221
dreams and dream journals, 181–182
duende, 174–176
Dulsky, Danielle, 177–178
dumb supper, 169
Dylan, Bob, 145, 175

earth
  about, 115–116
  asking permission and reciprocity and, 118–120
  associations and, 46
  calling a circle and, 43–44
  introduction to, 42
  metaphorical gifts from, 125–130
  music/songs of, 140–146
  poetry and, 131–134, 135–140
  ritual and, 120–123, 124–125, 135–140
  on Word Witch altar, 116–118, 124
  Word Witches as stewards of, 146–147
earth signs, 197
"Earth Teaches Me How to Keep a Secret, The," 243
"Earth That Listens to the Moon," 225
elegy, crafting, 166–169
"Elegy for Grandma Joan, An," 168
elements
  associations and, 44–47
  calling a circle and, 47–51
  introduction to, 42–43
  Word Witches and, 43–44
  See also individual elements
Elliott, Ramblin' Jack, 145
Emerson, Ralph Waldo, 133–134
energy, calling back, 251–253
Enheduanna, 157–159
"Equal Shadow That Casts Itself Across the Land," 139
equinoxes, 105, 106–107, 109
Estés, Clarissa Pinkola, 84, 88
Even Cowgirls Get the Blues (Robbins), 9–10
"Exaltation of Inanna, The," 158
expectations, 17

fairies, notes to, 3
fairy stones, 117–118
Fast Speaking Woman (Waldman), 145
fifth element, 151
Finch, Annie, 144–145
Fingernail of Luck, The (Hilberry), 128
fire
  about, 75–78
  associations and, 45
  Baba Yaga and, 80
  calling a circle and, 43–44
  inner light and, 86–88
  introduction to, 42
  play with, 85–86
  ritual and, 79–80
  on Word Witch altar, 78–79
fire signs, 197

first quarter moon, 102, 108
fixed signs, 197
Flowering Wand, The (Strand), 166
foundation
  altars and, 34–37, 39–40
  blessing of beginning for, 39–40
  calling a circle and, 47–51
  elements and, 42–44
  magical, 42–43
  as meeting point, 36
  physical, 34–37
  role of, 33–34
  sacred spaces and, 37–39
  of writing practice, 51–53
Four Elements of the Wise, The (Dominguez), 151
Franklin, Aretha, 175
freewriting, 91
Fuji, 89
full moon, 103, 109, 223–236
"Full Moon of My Lion Heart," 228
"Full Moon of Tender Lessons," 229
"Full Moon, the Earth Is Humming," 233

Gay, Ross, 66, 123
Gemini, 45, 197, 202–203, 226, 240
Ghost Ranch, 37
gifts of earth, 116–118, 125
Girmay, Aracelis, 26, 140
giveaways, 119
Glück, Louise, 127, 128
Gottesdiener, Sarah Faith, 100
gratitude, 69, 71–72, 109, 119
grief, 166–169
Grief Spells with Mara June, 167
Grossman, Pam, 13
Groundhog's Day, 111

hagstones, 118
Halloween, 109–110
hands, empty, 171–173
Harjo, Joy, 145
harvest
  first, 108
  second, 109
Hilberry, Conrad, 54–55, 128
"Horizon, Spring Arrives in the East, A," 137
How to Scan a Poem (Finch), 145
Howe, Marie, 66, 132

"I Take My Pen and I Put It to Paper," 203
illumination, 76, 77–79, 80–85. *See also* fire
"I'm Nobody! Who Are You?" (Dickinson), 2
imagination, 4, 11, 78, 85, 86
"Imagination Is a Form of Wintering," 246
Imbolc, 111–112
Inanna, 158
inner light, 86–88
inspiration, 76, 77–78, 175–176
intentions, 31–32, 52, 68, 92, 184, 194
interactive poetry prompts, 26
intuition, 27, 70, 79, 84, 92, 105, 108, 110
Isis, 177
"I—Toward a Definition" (Notley), 66

Joplin, Janis, 175
journals
  air magic and, 64–65
  choosing, 51–52
  fire and, 79–80

naming and reclamation and, 55
prompts for, 57–58, 74, 94, 113, 148, 185
water magic and, 99
judgment, 93

Kahlo, Frida, 38
Kalahari Desert, 40–41
Kapil, Bhanu, 129–130
Keats, John, 159–160
Kimmerer, Robin Wall, 118, 120
King, Stephen, 15
Klein, Bobby, 77

La Fortuna waterfall, 96–97
Langs' Fairy Books, 156
Lascaux Caves, 76
last quarter moon, 104, 111
Leo, 45, 197, 206–207, 228, 242
Letters to a Young Poet (Rilke), 55–56
"Letting Go My Hands Not Tightly Grasping," 209
Levin, Dana, 146
Libra, 45, 109, 197, 210–211, 230, 244
liminal space, 176–180
lineage, author's, 17–18
Lisenby, Kristin, 16, 53, 87, 161
Lorca, Federico Garcia, 174
Lughnasadh, 108–109

Mabon, 109
Magic School Bus, The, 28
Magick & Alchemy (podcast), 16, 161
Major Arcana: Portraits of Witches in America (Denny), 12–13
Marshall Public Library, 2
Meador, Betty De Shong, 159
meals, as offerings, 169–170
Mercury, 44
meter, 144
Missing Witches (Dickens and Torok), 8, 10
Mitchell, Joni, 145, 175
moon
cycles of, 101–105
as guide, 101
water and, 100
"Moon and Fire Both Know Change, The," 224
Moon Book, The (Gottesdiener), 100
"Moon Is Ancient, She Sings an Old Song, The," 234
Morrison, Van, 90, 175
movement, 85–86
music
feeling from, 140–141
incorporating into writing, 144–146
poetry and, 141–142, 145
songs of the earth, 140–144
mutable signs, 197
My So-Called Life, 152
Mystery Cult (Garcia), 30–31
"Myth of My Life, I Put My Pen to Paper," 239

naming and reclamation, 54–55
NASA, 96
nature, as oracle, 122
new moon, 101–102, 106, 107, 111, 237–250
Notley, Alice, 66, 181

offerings, 165–166, 169–170
O'Keeffe, Georgia, 37
Olive Fairy Book, The, 156
Oliver, Mary, 121, 123

INDEX

"On Wings I Travel to Horizons," 226
On Writing (King), 15
oneiromancy, 181
Orr, Gregory, 141
Overstory, The (Powers), 61

page, as altar, 28
permission, asking, 118–120, 124
persistence, 150
Pierce Cedar Creek Institute, 127–128
Pisces, 46, 197, 220–221, 235–236, 249–250
planchette writing, 89
Plath, Sylvia, 161
play, 85–86
"Plum Trees, The" (Oliver), 121
Pluma, 77
"Poet, The" (Emerson), 133–134
poetry
  about, 131–134
  author's first, 5
  elegies and, 166–169
  interactive prompts for, 26
  music and, 141–142, 145
  ritual and, 135–140
  travel and, 122
  See also prompts
Poetry Foundation, 65
possibility, 7, 25
Powers, Richard, 61
Practical Magic, 47
preconceived notions, 53–54
presence, radical, 122
Princess, Priestess, Poet (Meador), 159
prompts
  astrological season, 197–221
  for blessing, 72
  full moon, 223–236
  new moon, 237–250
  for poetry, 135–139
  for reflection, 125
  for Word Witch journal, 57–58, 74, 94, 113, 148, 185
psychography. *See* automatic writing

"Quiver of Fire, A," 232

rain cycle, 97–98
reciprocity, 118–120, 124, 171
reclamation, naming and, 54–55
Refuge (Williams), 61
"Renewal Comes in Many Forms," 247
rhyme schemes, 70, 144
Rilke, Rainer Maria, 55–56
rituals
  air magic, 64–65
  automatic writing, 88–93
  calling upon cycles, 100–101
  calling your energy back, 251–253
  cord-cutting release ritual, 53–54
  crafting and elegy, 166–169
  earth magic, 124–125
  fire magic, 79–80
  gratitude and blessing as a spell, 71–72
  importance of, 40–41
  naming and reclamation, 54–55
  offering attention, 120–123
  offerings and, 169–170
  saying yes to Word Witch path, 55–56
  spirit and, 179–180, 182–184
  steps to creating, 193–195
  threshold, 179–180
  water magic, 99–100

writing a poem, 135–140
Robbins, Tom, 9–10
roots, 130, 175, 178
Ruiz, Felicia Cocotzin, 118
Rukeyser, Muriel, 10

Sabina, Maria, 145
sacred spaces, 37–39
Sagittarius, 45, 197, 214–215, 232, 246
Samhain, 106, 109–110, 178
Santayana, George, 140
Sappho, 161
Sargon the Great, 158
"Scales Dance in Balance, The," 230
"Scales That Bring Changes Are Always in Balance," 244
scansion, 144–145
Scorpio, 46, 110, 197, 212–213, 231, 245
"Season of Slowness, I Reach My Hands Up, The," 201
seasonal cycles, 105–112
seasons
  astrological, 197–221
  as gifts, 130
  observing, 193
  poetry prompts and, 135–139
self, authentic, 152
"Self-Portrait," 153–154
Seuss, Diane, 128, 174
Shakespeare, William, 140
Smith, Heidi, 96
solstices, 105, 108, 110–111
soul lanterns, 87–88
spell crafting, 67–70
Spiral Dance, The (Starhawk), 21, 86
spirit
  about, 149–152
  ancestors and, 153–165
  associations and, 46–47
  duende and, 174–176
  empty hands and, 171–173
  introduction to, 42
  ritual and, 166–170, 179–180, 182–184
  thresholds and, 176–180
  on Word Witch altar, 161–165
spirit writing. *See* automatic writing
spiritualism, 90
spring equinox, 106–107, 178
"Stand of Pines, A," 142–143
Starhawk, 21, 86
starlings, 62–63
"Start of a Cycle, We Begin Again, The," 199, 238
"Still, the Sun Rises," 205
stillness, seeking, 120–121
stories/storytelling, 1, 3, 10, 11, 84–85, 151–152, 154, 156–157, 160, 177–178
Strand, Sophie, 166
subconscious, 100, 104, 169
Suler, Asia, 118
"Summer Is a Spiral, as Most Things Are," 138
summer solstice, 108
"Sun Speaks," 207
Surrealist Manifesto (Breton), 90
surrealist movement, 90
symbolic actions, 30–31

Tamed Wild, 16, 87
Taurus, 46, 197, 200–201, 225, 239
"Thank You" (Gay), 66
"Theory and Play of Duende, The" (Lorca), 174
"This Living Hand" (Keats), 160

"Threshold of Winter, on the Altar I Offer This Poem," 217
thresholds, 176–180
time travel, 5
Torok, Amy, 8, 10
trees, 61, 77
turkey vultures, 61–62

Vasilisa, 80–85
veils, 176–179
Viray, Xenia, 98
Virgo, 46, 197, 208–209, 229, 243
Voicing the Natural (Belew), 127–128

Waal, Edmund de, 66
Waits, Tom, 175
Waking the Witch (Grossman), 13
Waldman, Anne, 145
waning crescent, 104–105, 111
waning gibbous, 103–104, 110
water
  about, 95–98
  associations and, 45–46
  calling a circle and, 43–44
  introduction to, 42
  ritual and, 99–101
  on Word Witch altar, 98–99, 170
water signs, 197
"Water That Pools in My Heart," 213
"Waters of Change," 227
waxing crescent, 102, 107
waxing gibbous, 103, 109
"We Real Cool" (Brooks), 145–146
"We Were Made for These Times" (Estés), 88
"What Is Ancient Has Always Loved the Moon," 245
"What the Living Do" (Howe), 66
Wheel of the Year, 105
"Where There Is Water, There Must Be Tides," 249–250
Whitman, Walt, 135
Wild Iris, The (Glück), 127
Williams, Terry Tempest, 61
"Winds of Change That Blow Back," 219
winter solstice, 110–111
"Winter Still Lingers Its Cold Against My Skin," 248
witches, defining, 8–9
Women Who Run with the Wolves (Estés), 84
Woolley, Leonard, 157
Word Witches
  defining, 12–13
  as earth stewards, 146–147
  elements and, 43–44
  guiding beliefs of, 14
  saying yes to path of, 55–56
  spiral path of, 21
  use of book and, 19–20
  See also individual people
"Woven, the Season of Solstice Offers Threads," 140
writer's block, 171, 173
writing ritual, steps to creating, 193–195

Yates Garcia, Amanda, 10, 30–31
Young, Neil, 175

ABOUT THE AUTHOR

Kate Belew is a writer, poet, and Witch. Her work exists at the crossroads of creativity and magic. She has taught and facilitated circles and workshops worldwide since 2017. She is dedicated to the spirit of poetry and the sacred wild of the planet and seeks enchantment in all she does. She is a forever student of the plants and the stars. She has an MFA in writing from Sarah Lawrence College. Her roots are in Michigan, and her wings are in Brooklyn, two places she calls home.

RAISING READERS

Books Build Bright Futures

hank you for reading this book and for being a reader of books in general. As an uthor, I am so grateful to share being part of a community of readers with you, nd I hope you will join me in passing our love of books on to the next generation f readers.

id you know that reading for enjoyment is the single biggest predictor of a hild's future happiness and success?

ore than family circumstances, parents' educational background, or income, eading impacts a child's future academic performance, emotional well-being, ommunication skills, economic security, ambition, and happiness.

tudies show that kids reading for enjoyment in the US is in rapid decline:

- In 2012, 53% of 9-year-olds read almost every day. Just 10 years later, in 2022, the number had fallen to 39%.
- In 2012, 27% of 13-year-olds read for fun daily. By 2023, that number was just 14%.

Together, we can commit to **Raising Readers** and change this trend. How?

- Read to children in your life daily.
- Model reading as a fun activity.
- Reduce screen time.
- Start a family, school, or community book club.
- Visit bookstores and libraries regularly.
- Listen to audiobooks.
- Read the book before you see the movie.
- Encourage your child to read aloud to a pet or stuffed animal.
- Give books as gifts.
- Donate books to families and communities in need.

BOB1217

Books build bright futures, and **Raising Readers** is our shared responsibility.

For more information, visit **JoinRaisingReaders.com**

Sources: National Endowment for the Arts, National Assessment of Educational Progress, WorldBookDay.org, Nielsen BookData's 2023 "Understanding the Children's Book Consumer"